# THE WORKING LIFE

# A Sweatshop During the Industrial Revolution

## TITLES IN THE WORKING LIFE SERIES INCLUDE:

# THE WORKING LIFE

# A Sweatshop During the Industrial Revolution

ADAM WOOG

LUCENT
BOOKS ®

THOMSON
————————————
GALE

San Diego • Detroit • New York • San Francisco • Cleveland • New Haven, Conn. • Waterville, Maine • London • Munich

Thanks to Steve Long, curator of the Tenement Museum in New York City, and to Daniel Soyer, professor of history at Fordham University, for research advice and materials.

LIBRARY OF CONGRESS CATALOGING-IN-PUBLICATION DATA

Woog, Adam, 1953–
   A sweatshop during the industrial revolution / by Adam Woog.
      v. cm. — (The working life series)
Includes bibliographical references and index.
Contents: Who worked in sweatshops?—Daily life in a sweatshop—Dangers in the sweatshop—Life outside the sweatshop—The role of organized labor.
   ISBN 1-59018-179-4
   1. Sweatshops—United States—History—Juvenile literature. 2. Sweatshops—United States—Employees—Juvenile literature. [1. Sweatshops—History. 2. Industrial revolution—United States. 3. United States—Economic conditions—To 1865. 4. United States—Social conditions—To 1865.] I. Title. II. Series.
   HD2339.U6 W66 2003
   331.25—dc21
                                          2002005162

Printed in the United States of America

# CONTENTS

# FOREWORD

"The strongest bond of human sympathy outside the family relations should be one uniting all working people of all nations and tongues and kindreds."

Abraham Lincoln. 1864

Work is a common activity in which almost all people engage. It is probably the most universal of human experiences, the drive to work. As Henry Ford, inventor of the Model T said, "There will never be a system invented which will do away with the necessity of work." For many people, work takes up most of their day. They spend more time with their co-workers than family and friends. And the common goals people pursue on the job may be among the first thoughts that they have in the morning, and the last that they may have at night.

While the idea of work is universal, the way it is done and who performs it varies considerably throughout history. The story of work is inextricably tied to the history of technology, the history of culture, and the history of gender and race. When the typewriter was invented, for example, it was considered the exclusive domain of men who worked as secretaries. As women workers became more accepted, the secretarial role was gradually filled by women. Finally, with the invention of the computer, the modern secretary spends little time actually typing correspondence. Files are delivered via computer, and more time is spent on other tasks than the manual typing of correspondence and business.

This is just one example of how work brings together technology, gender, and culture. Another example is the American plantation slave. The harvesting of cotton was initially so cumbersome and time consuming that even with slaves, its profitability was doubtful. With the invention of the cotton gin, however, efficiency improved, and slavery became a viable agricultural tool. It also became a Southern tradition and institution, enough that the South was willing to go to war to preserve it.

The books in Lucent's Working Life series strive to show the intermingling of work, and its reflection in culture, technology, race, and gender. Indeed, history viewed through the lens of the average worker is both enlightening and fascinating. Take the history of the typewriter, mentioned above. Readers today have access to more technology than any of their historical counterparts, and, in fact, though they would find the typewriter's keyboard familiar, they would find using it a bore. Finding out that people spent their days sitting over that machine (with no talk of carpal tunnel syndrome!) and were valued if they made no typing errors because corrections were cumbersome to make and, in some legal professions, made documents invalid, is an interesting story that involves many different aspects of history.

The desire to work is almost innate. As German socialist Ferdinand Lassalle said in the 1850s, "Workingmen we all are so far as we have the desire to make ourselves useful to human society in any way whatever." Yet each historical period offers a million different stories of the history of each job and how it was performed. And that history is the history of human society.

Each book in the Working Life series strives to tell the tale of these anonymous workers. Primary source quotes offer veracity and immediacy to each volume, letting the workers themselves tell their stories. In addition, thorough bibliographies tell students where they can find out more information and complete indexes allow for easy perusal of the text. While students learn about the work of years gone by, they gain empathy for those that toil, and, perhaps, a universal pride in taking up the work that will someday be theirs.

# THE SWEATSHOP IN THE INDUSTRIAL REVOLUTION

Picture this dismal scene—a garment sweatshop, a small factory for making ready-to-wear clothing, as described by journalist Jacob Riis in 1890:

Up two flights of dark stairs, three, four, with new smells of cabbage, of onions, of frying fish, on every landing, whirring sewing machines behind closed doors betraying what goes on within, to the door that opens to admit the bundle [of cloth] and the man. . . . Five men and a woman, two young girls, not fifteen, and a boy who says unasked that he is fifteen, and lies in saying it, are at the machines sewing knickerbockers, "knee-pants.". . .

The floor is littered ankle-deep with half-sewn garments. In the alcove, on a couch of many dozens of "pants" ready for the finisher, a bare-legged baby with pinched face is asleep. A fence of piled-up clothing keeps him from rolling off on the floor. The faces, hands, and arms to the elbows of everyone in the room are black with the color of the cloth on which they are working.[1]

## A MULTITUDE OF SWEATSHOPS

Sweatshops like this one were common during the Industrial Revolution, the period when America and other countries shifted from being mostly rural and agricultural to being mostly urban and industrial. The peak years of sweatshops in America spanned roughly from 1880 to 1920, though in the United States and elsewhere sweatshops existed before then and have reappeared periodically since.

Sweatshops manufactured many different items, and sweatshop workers performed many different tasks. They sorted feathers to decorate ladies' hats. They glued paper petals onto stems to create artificial flowers. They made soap. They wrapped candy, rolled cigars, made boxes, or sorted and packed nuts or pickles.

The majority of sweatshops, however, were devoted to the creation of ready-to-wear clothing. Among the items they made for this huge industry were suits, ties, hats, underwear, shoes, blouses, skirts, dresses, gloves, shirts, cloaks, and coats.

Garment sweatshops existed in many of America's industrial cities,

## ❧ GRINDING OUT WORK ❧

*Journalist Ray Stannard Baker, in this excerpt from "Plight of the Tailors," a 1904 magazine article, summarizes the sweatshop experience:*

There are not many things that an unskilled foreigner, knowing no English, can do; but almost any man or woman can sew. And thus flourished the sweatshop, the home of the "task system," where men, women and children worked together in unhealthful, often diseased, and sometimes immoral surroundings. Nowhere in the world at any time, probably, were men and women worked as they were in the sweatshop—the lowest paid, most degrading of American employment. The sweatshop employer ground all the work he could from every man, woman and child under him.

*An early twentieth-century photo of a clothing factory shows the cramped and drab working conditions of the sweatshop.*

but New York City was the center of ready-to-wear manufacturing. As of 1910 New York had roughly thirty thousand garment sweatshops that employed half a million workers. Together, these shops produced 70 percent of all the women's clothing and 40 percent of all the men's clothing in America.

## "A State of Mind"

Often, sweatshops were simply private apartments, the homes of business owners who used their own living spaces as small factories. Such tiny operations might employ half a dozen workers. Sometimes, sweatshops were set up in slightly larger spaces, such as in the basements of apartment buildings. Such medium-sized shops typically had twenty or twenty-five employees. And sometimes sweatshops were larger operations, employing several hundred people in buildings specifically built for factory work.

No matter the size, and no matter what they produced, sweatshops were dismal and oppressive places in which to work. They were cramped, filthy,

*Child laborers sew garments. Immigrant children provided an abundant supply of cheap labor to sweatshops across the United States.*

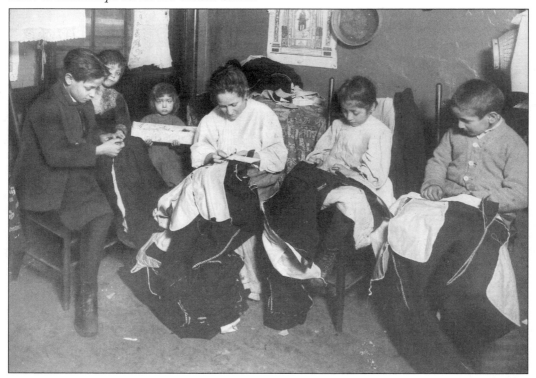

## ❧ BIG CHANGES ☙

*In this passage from* We Were There: The Story of Working Women in America, *historian Barbara Mayer Wertheimer summarizes some of the massive transformations America was undergoing during the Industrial Revolution. These changes were both good and bad for working-class sweatshop employees:*

By 1880 the United States had become the world's leading industrial nation. . . . It could hardly keep up with the rapid growth in population, the rush to its cities with new inventions like the electric light, the telephone, the transatlantic telegraph, the typewriter. Railroads crisscrossed the country. Steel mills belched smoke day and night. Electricity was applied to industry: transformers, dynamos, motors. An age of specialization began: some stores sold meat, others candy, others baked goods. Canning of meats and vegetables was introduced. So were the department store, standardized packaging of goods, and brand-name advertising.

Rapidly growing cities meant more slums, filled by the numbers of immigrants, almost half a million a year now, who came to America to start a new life and provided a never-ending supply of cheap labor for the giant firms that made a few Americans very rich. This was the day of the "robber barons," the railroad, steel, and mining magnates whose lives contrasted so sharply with those of the average working men and women their empires employed.

and poorly lit. They were frequently dangerous as well; accidents and the spread of disease were commonplace. Furthermore, sweatshop workers performed their dull routine tasks for long hours and low pay with little ability to control—much less improve—their situations.

These appalling conditions had such a profound impact on millions of workers, and on society in general, that sweatshops have become enduring symbols for any kind of demeaning, exhausting, and abusive work. In the words of historian Leon Stein, "The sweatshop is a state of mind as well as a physical fact."[2]

## DISPOSABLE PARTS

The Industrial Revolution was the period that introduced to the world mechanical power for manufacturing, industry, and mass production of goods. The new machines and processes of the era were wondrous—and wondrously productive. Machines powered by steam, electricity, or coal changed forever the ways in which everything from dresses to steel to guns could be made.

Machines could do only part of the work, however. People were still needed to run and maintain the equipment. Furthermore, the human touch was still required to complete important parts of the process. Shops thus arose that used human workers as if they were disposable "parts" of a larger piece of machinery, "sweating" the most work out of them for the least amount of money possible. These minifactories became known as sweatshops. Despite the terrible working conditions, sweatshops were never short of employees because they provided the only jobs available to millions of people during the Industrial Revolution.

The "disposable" workers who labored in sweatshops came from many places. Typically, they were unskilled; the majority were women and children. Millions were recent immigrants. All of them were bound together by the sweatshop experience—an experience that was awful in many ways, but which kept them employed and even held out occasional glimmers of pleasure.

# CHAPTER 1

# WHO WORKED IN SWEATSHOPS?

The enormous numbers of people needed to run sweatshops was provided primarily by immigrant women and children, who flooded America's sweatshops, eager for work. The arrival in this country between 1871 and 1911 of some 20.5 million Europeans and Russians constituted one of the most dramatic population changes in modern times. These workers came in such vast numbers that journalist Jacob Riis wrote in 1890 that "the supply across the sea is apparently inexhaustible."[3]

They may have dreamed of something grander, but for millions of immigrants the only jobs available to them were in sweatshops. Sweatshops became so closely linked to the immigrant experience, labor organizer Joseph Schlossberg noted, that for these new arrivals "the sweatshop *was* America."[4]

## ESCAPE FROM POVERTY

Jews from Russia and eastern Europe and Italians were the two largest ethnic groups of immigrants during this period. Sizable numbers of other subgroups, including Poles, Germans, Greeks, and Slovaks, rounded out the influx of new arrivals. Some came to America because they were fleeing

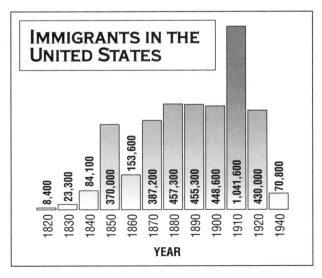

**IMMIGRANTS IN THE UNITED STATES**

| YEAR | Number |
| --- | --- |
| 1820 | 8,400 |
| 1830 | 23,300 |
| 1840 | 84,100 |
| 1850 | 370,000 |
| 1860 | 153,600 |
| 1870 | 387,200 |
| 1880 | 457,300 |
| 1890 | 455,300 |
| 1900 | 448,600 |
| 1910 | 1,041,600 |
| 1920 | 430,000 |
| 1940 | 70,800 |

## ❧ OVERNIGHT MILLIONAIRES ❧

*Marcus Ravage, in this passage from Irving Howe and Kenneth Libo's* How We Lived: A Documentary History of Immigrant Jews in America 1880–1930, *recalls that everyone in his native Romania was full of tales of the splendid life they would find in America as immigrants:*

In the year of my departure from Rumania in 1900 America had become, as it were, the fashionable place to go. . . . All my relatives and all our neighbors—in fact, everybody who was any-body—had either gone or was going to New York.

Everybody who went there became a millionaire overnight, and a doctor or a teacher into the bargain. In New York, it appeared, education was to be got altogether without cost. . . . The government of America not only did not exact charges for instruction; it compelled parents to send their children to school, and it begged grown-ups to come and be educated when their day's work was over. There, in America, was my future, as well as my family's.

religious prejudice or political oppression in their homeland. Many were simple, uneducated working-class people or farm laborers.

Almost all hoped to escape lives of poverty and desperation. They traveled with a mixture of emotions: fear of the unknown, relief and sadness at leaving, concern and hope about what was to come. One woman recalled sailing to America as a young child: "We went third class, with the poverty-stricken, but it was lively, everybody talking and looking forward to God knows what kind of future it was going to be."[5]

Having spent their life savings to buy passage by ship, they arrived with little more than what they could carry. Many came through America's main immigration portal, Ellis Island in New York harbor. There they were thoroughly checked to ensure they had proper papers and healthy bodies. Those who did not pass inspection were turned back. The portal thus took on near-magical proportions for immigrants, since it symbolized the passage to a hopeful new life or the return to a despairing old one. A journalist of the period describes this scene aboard a ship coming into the harbor:

"There is Ellis Island!" shouted an immigrant who had already been in the United States. . . . The name acted like magic. Faces grew taut, eyes narrowed. There, in those red buildings, fate awaited them.

Were they ready to enter? Or were they to be sent back? "Only God knows," shouted an elderly man, his withered hand gripping the railing.[6]

## "DE ODER SIDE"

Sometimes whole families came together. Often, however, an immigrant family arrived in bits and pieces. The head of a family or an unmarried brother might come by himself first and find work, saving every penny until he could afford to send back passage for others. As more family members arrived, they likewise found work and contributed to the shared family income. Any extra money was sent back to "the old country" to support remaining relatives or buy passage for them.

In this way many immigrants began to feel they were in America long before they actually arrived. This attitude is echoed in an old joke from the Jewish vaudeville theater: In reply to the question "Are you a foreigner?" the answer was: "No, I'm an American from de oder side."[7]

Once through the gates at Ellis Island, immigrants found themselves in a strange new world. Many of these

*Newly arrived immigrants file through the lines of Ellis Island on their way to what they hope will be a better life.*

people had never been out of their small home villages, and New York was a startling revelation. Rose Cohen, who came from Russia as a young girl, describes her feelings when she first arrived: "I was dazed by all there was to see. I looked with wonder at the tall houses, the paved streets, the street lamps. As I had never seen a large city and only had had a glimpse of a small one, I thought these things true only of America."[8]

Some immigrants headed to the open country of the West, looking for farmland and adventure. However, the vast majority of them settled in Boston, New York, Chicago, Detroit, and other industrialized cities of the Northeast and Midwest.

## NEW YORK CITY

Millions of the new arrivals got no further than New York City. This was especially true of the eastern European Jews. Historian Moses Rischin notes, "For East Europeans of the great Jewish migration New York was the promised city. There most of them were to find their first American employment and strike permanent roots."[9]

*An immigrant family gazes at the Statue of Liberty, the most powerful symbol of American freedom and opportunity.*

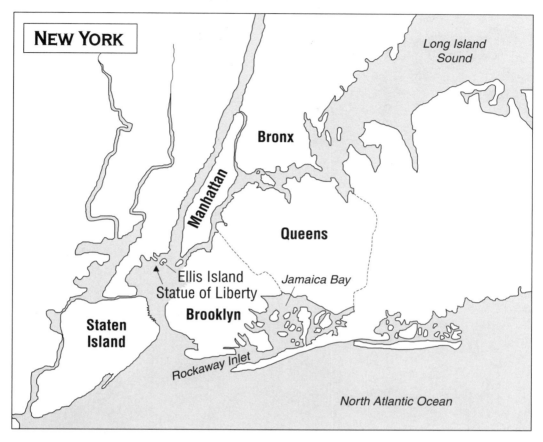

For many immigrants, their new life was an exciting dream—at least at first. America, the land of opportunity, offered the chance to make a fresh start. Writer and social worker Frederic C. Howe noted in 1905, "The [American] city is El Dorado, the promised land which fires the imagination. Failure may come, it is true, but there is the chance, and life, movement, and recreation even in failure."[10]

Eager to work, immigrants looked for jobs wherever they could. They found them in a variety of settings, including bakeries, restaurants, street peddling, laboring, and, especially, in sweatshops. Of all the trades, New York's garment industry with its thousands of tiny shops provided a niche immigrants could easily fill. They were initially hired on as "greenhorns"—that is, new and untried workers. As journalist Ray Stannard Baker put it in 1904, "There are not many things that an unskilled foreigner, knowing no English, can do; but almost any man or woman can sew."[11]

*New York City's Herald Square brims with activity in this photo from 1908. This lively scene stands in stark contrast to the squalid existence of the typical immigrant.*

## NEW WORK AND LIFE

Many immigrants eagerly embraced the American dream and hoped to be quickly assimilated—that is, American-ized. They wanted to abandon their old customs, learn English, and acquire American friends and manners. Life was good to them in their new home, compared to the dire poverty they had known before coming. Historians Oscar Theodore Barck Jr. and Nelson Manfred Blake remark, "By comparison with Europe . . . the United States was a land of good wages and advantageous working conditions."[12]

However, some found that life in America could be harsh. These new arrivals discovered that the grim cycles of poverty, prejudice, and illness they had left behind were simply repeated in their new homes. Perhaps these new homes were not as fine as promised, either; one immigrant woman responded disgustedly to seeing the gloomy, decaying apartment she was expected to live in: "So we have crossed half the world for this!"[13]

Furthermore, daily life in America was frequently strange and intimidating, especially for someone far from familiar surroundings and who spoke little if any English. It was a shock for a reasonably well-educated person to suddenly become a functional illiterate in a new country. Furthermore, the tempo of a big city could easily unset-

tle someone used to life in a small village. One immigrant recalled,

My home, my school, the food, the city in itself. I just didn't know how to cope with it all. I was unhappy because I didn't understand the language. I sort of felt that I was a big shot student in Russia. And here I didn't know anything and I was frightened. Two days after I came off the

*This late nineteenth-century photo of a New York apartment courtyard reveals the overcrowded, dirty conditions in which many American immigrants lived.*

boat, my father enrolled me in school, and that was the worst time.

When they used to call me names like "greenhorn," I felt that I would rather die than hear it again. There were times I wished that they would send me back to my grandfather. I would have rather been without my parents than be here.[14]

## ETHNIC TENSIONS AND BIGOTRY

As more and more immigrants arrived, some native-born Americans grew wary. They feared the foreigners' customs and religions and worried that their jobs were being stolen by the new arrivals. Several attempts were made to pass legislation to stop or slow the flood of immigration. Historian Frank Freidel notes, "Many Americans . . . were susceptible to the

*An Italian immigrant smokes a pipe amid the squalor of his makeshift home.*

popular dogma [belief] of Anglo-Saxon superiority, and joined in the anti-immigration movement."[15] Even Theodore Roosevelt, president of the United States from 1901 to 1909 and a generally tolerant man, warned darkly against "race suicide."

Furthermore, tension among immigrant groups themselves often ran high. In part this was because some groups, notably the Irish, Germans, and Scandinavians, were already well established. These groups frequently looked down with scorn on new arrivals. The established immigrant groups were more affluent, spoke better English, and understood better the ways of their adopted home.

Sometimes bigotry existed within individual ethnic groups; already established Jews from Germany and Holland, for instance, often regarded newly arrived eastern European Jews with scorn. New arrivals, with their limited language abilities and social and work skills, were nothing more than lowly "greenhorn" employees. Their rough, uneducated ways, according to historian Moses Rischin, "seemed to threaten [the established immigrants'] hard-won respectability."[16]

## WOMEN AND CHILDREN

Immigrant men were by no means the only people who found work in sweatshops. Women and children, both immigrant and native-born, were just as important in the sweatshop labor force.

Women and children, however, were hired according to a strict hierarchy. Almost invariably they were allowed to take on only the least desirable, lowest-paid work; the better positions went primarily to men. Lottie Spitzer, a Chicago coat-factory worker, recalls, "That's the way it was, men sitting by the big jobs and women by the little jobs."[17]

One reason for this difference was that few women had work experience other than home and child care, so a lack of skills severely limited their opportunities. Despite this lack, many women did join the workforce during the Industrial Revolution; by 1900 one-fifth of the manufacturing labor force in America was female.

Many people of the period believed that women worked primarily just to supplement their husbands' or fathers' income with a little extra money. In fact, women often provided significant portions of their family's budget, and sometimes they were the family's sole support. In 1911 activist Elizabeth Dutcher wrote that the unmarried immigrant women she knew "were supporting old fathers and mothers, both in this country and abroad; mothering and supporting younger brothers and sisters, sending brothers to high school, to art school, to dental college, to engineering courses."[18]

Despite the fact that they had access to only the lowliest positions, many women were grateful simply to have

*Seamstresses manufacture garments in a clothing factory. As part of an assembly line, the sweatshop seamstress performed the same task over and over.*

jobs. The concept of working outside the house was still a relatively new and daring one for many, especially if they came from rural or conservative backgrounds that frowned on women in the workplace.

For many, therefore, even the worst job represented a degree of freedom. One woman, identified only as Tanya N., recalled, "Work was success. As long as I was working at something that was paying a salary, my father wouldn't have to support me. My mother was helping my father. If she could take care of a house and five kids, then I could work. And I wanted to work to help out."[19]

## ASSEMBLY LINE SEAMSTRESSES

Many women of the time found jobs, such as teaching or secretarial work, that were not part of the sweatshop experience. Most, however, found they were obliged to work in fields that did rely heavily on sweatshops. Among these were textile manufacture, food packing, or the creation of small items such as cigars or artificial flowers.

Generally, the easiest place of all for women to find work was in the garment industry. This was because most women had at least a basic knowledge of sewing. Even if a woman had no other marketable skills and spoke virtually no English, she could usually find work in a garment sweatshop.

Here as elsewhere, men still took the more skilled jobs such as cutting pieces of cloth, or those that required greater physical strength such as lifting the heavy irons used for pressing clothes. Most of the remaining jobs for adults in garment sweatshops were as seamstresses, a broad term that covered several categories.

Unlike a dressmaker—a skilled worker who custom-made entire garments—a seamstress did not create whole items. Instead, she was merely part of an assembly line team and performed one task over and over, such as sewing on buttons. She simply received partially finished garments from one person, performed her particular task, and passed the garments on to the next. Writer Louise C. Odencrantz reported in 1919, "Unfortunately they [immigrant women] have no realization of the fine subdivisions that exist in the trade today, when such tasks as sewing on buttons on shirtwaists, cutting threads off petticoats, operating a ruffling or buttonhole machine, or setting in sleeves may be the one process that a girl will work at year after year."[20]

## ❧ MADAME'S WORKSHOP ❧

*Most sweatshop bosses were men, but not all. Wert Sikes, a prominent New York City social reformer, wrote this passage in 1868 describing a woman-owned garment sweatshop. It is reprinted in Cornell University Library's website exhibit* The Triangle Factory Fire:

There are some roomy and cheerful shops in the city. But there are scores, and hundreds, that are not roomy and cheerful. The worst of these are owned and conducted by women. . . .

This is the workroom. Faugh, how it smells! There is no attempt at ventilation. The room is crowded with girls and women, most of whom are pale and attenuated, and are being robbed of life slowly and surely. The rose which should bloom in their cheeks has vanished long ago. The sparkle has gone out of their eyes. They bend over their work with aching backs and throbbing brows; sharp pains dart through their eyeballs; they breathe an atmosphere of death.

Madame pays her girls four dollars a week. She herself lives in as fine a style as the richest lady she serves.

## CHILD LABOR

Children were the third major component of the sweatshop workforce. It was commonplace for children to work right alongside grown women and men, in sweatshops and elsewhere, during this period in history. The concept of children working alongside adults was nothing new. For thousands of years children had begun their working lives at an age that today seems shocking. Before the Industrial Revolution, for instance, boys and girls routinely began helping out with the family farm's or business's chores almost as soon as they could walk. Boys typically were apprenticed to craftsmen at the age of ten or even younger.

It is not surprising, therefore, that when the Industrial Revolution arrived child labor was an integral part of the sweatshop, that it was an accepted part of life almost everywhere, and that few laws existed to regulate unfair or exploitative cases. Jacob Riis noted in 1890 that in sweatshops "the child works unchallenged from the day he is old enough to pull a thread."[21]

Children performed a variety of jobs in sweatshops, many of them as complex—and certainly as dull—as the jobs adults were doing. At a typical shirtwaist factory, for instance, they sorted buttons, threaded needles, and ran errands such as delivering bundles. They also rolled cigars, made artificial flowers, and performed similar menial tasks in a variety of settings.

Owners of sweatshops liked to hire children for several reasons. For one thing, children accepted even lower wages than adult sweatshop workers. Also the smaller, more agile hands and bodies of children were preferred for certain delicate jobs such as performing maintenance on textile machinery. Furthermore, children were less likely than adults to complain about substandard working conditions.

## AVOIDING THE LAW

Almost no laws significantly restricted shop owners from hiring young children, overworking them, or letting them perform dangerous work. Any laws that did exist, furthermore, were easy to ignore or cover up—something that a child certainly went along with if he or she wanted to avoid getting fired.

Laws were especially easy to circumvent if a child worked in a tenement sweatshop, a small shop that was an outgrowth of a family home in a slum apartment. There, children as young as five routinely worked fourteen to eighteen hours a day, helping their mothers and fathers roll cigars, stitch clothing, or do other small-scale jobs. Labor inspectors rarely bothered to visit such makeshift home factories; when they did, it was easy for children to hide or pretend they were not working.

In a letter to relatives written years later, Pauline Newman recalled her childhood in a garment sweatshop. She

*Garment workers, including a young boy, take a short break. Child labor was an integral part of the sweatshop.*

noted that finished shirtwaists (ladies' blouses) were stored in cases, ready for examination by inspectors, and came in very handy for children on the job as well as their bosses:

> By the way, these cases were used for another purpose which served the employers very well indeed. [They] were high enough and deep enough for us kids to hide in, so that when a factory inspector came to inspect the factory he found no violation of the child labor law, because he did not see any children at work—we were all hidden in the cases and covered with shirtwaists!

> Clever of them, was it not? Somehow the employers seemed to have known when the inspector would come and had time enough to arrange for our hiding place.[22]

## MIRED

Some sweatshop workers prospered. Immigrants saved enough to bring relatives over. Women were able to open their own businesses or find better work. Children reached adulthood, started families, and saved enough to start their own children on the road to a better life than they themselves had experienced.

However, such success stories were not always the case. No matter whether a worker was a man, woman, or child, it seemed at times virtually impossible to get ahead in a sweatshop. The wages were so low, and the hours so long, that most could barely survive. In 1913 a seventeen-year-old Russian identified only as "K.A." told a reporter,

"My father saved enough money to bring mother and me to America. He came here first and worked to save the money; but the long hours and poor food made him a nervous wreck, and then mother and me had to support him. Then mother broke down altogether and I had to support them both."[23]

K.A.'s story is all too typical. Some who spent time in the sweatshops used them simply as stepping stones to something better. Others, however, remained sweatshop workers for the rest of their lives, trapped in an endlessly repeating daily cycle of spirit-dulling work.

# CHAPTER 2

# DAILY LIFE IN A SWEATSHOP

Daily life in a sweatshop was almost relentlessly grim. The atmosphere was dirty, gloomy, boring, and sometimes noisy. It was, moreover, often dangerous; workers were subject to overwork, abuse, and exhaustion. Garment worker Pauline Newman recalled, "Someone once asked me: 'How did you survive?' And I told him, what alternative did we have? You stayed and you survived, that's all." [24]

Nonetheless, some sweatshops managed to maintain an air of friendship and camaraderie. Since workers frequently labored in close proximity to people from their home villages and others with similar backgrounds and interests, sweatshops could be amiable and even intellectually stimulating. The daily life of a sweatshop worker could also contain occasional bursts of optimism, hope, and cheer.

## THE SIZE OF A SHOP
The number of sweatshop workers in a given shop varied greatly. Some small shops had only four employees in a single basement room. Others might have twenty or thirty people in what had once been a three-room apartment. Still larger shops employed several hundred people and occupied multiple floors of factory buildings. The majority of sweatshops, those for the garment trade, were small; historian Moses Rischin writes, "In no other industry could so many shops numbering so few employees be found." [25]

Four was the minimum for a team of garment workers. Production of almost any piece of clothing required a baster (who did the initial preparation, fitting and lightly sewing pieces of cloth together by hand), a sewing machine operator (who sewed these pieces together), a finisher or trimmer (who made finishing touches by hand),

*This early twentieth-century photo depicts the operation of a small garment sweatshop with six employees.*

and a presser (who pressed the finished work with heavy irons).

Many shops employed two basting/sewing/finishing teams, since they could keep one presser busy. Some shops hired extra finishers for more complicated work such as adding lace to a collar. Larger shops preferred to hire cutters to cut out pieces of cloth from whole bolts, rather than use pre-cut (and more expensive) pieces.

One or two workers, often children, were also employed in a typical shop, for running odd jobs such as carrying bundles or partially completed garments from one sweatshop to another for the next steps. In addition, there were often occasional part-time employees or employees who worked at home. A typical mid-sized garment sweatshop usually had eight or nine employees, although (counting everyone on both ends of the production process) it was not unusual for a single shirt or blouse to pass through twenty or thirty pairs of hands before completion.

Within the shops themselves, workers sat in various configurations for maximum efficiency. Larger garment shops, for instance, usually had cutters in one room and sewing machine operators in another. The sewing machine operators sat in long, tightly packed rows, back to back. Historian Daniel Soyer writes that a typical small garment sweatshop also had a strict hierarchy:

> The operators' foot-powered machines stood by the windows of the front room, where the only natural light entered the apartment. The basters sat on chairs to the side. The finishers sat on the floor or on the piles of goods that littered the room, while the pressers worked on tables set up in the kitchen, where they heated the irons on the stove. The pressers worked by gaslight, since the interior tenement rooms usually had no windows. [26]

## CROWDED, DIM, DIRTY

No matter how many workers were employed in a given sweatshop, it always seemed crowded. Every inch of available space was taken up with

*A family sews together around the kitchen table in a tenement sweatshop. Many immigrant families converted their slum apartments into such sweatshops.*

people, machines, and raw material. Sometimes rooms were especially crowded because they were also living quarters. Jacob Riis noted, "It is not unusual to find a dozen persons— men, women, and children—at work in a single small room. . . . Every member of the family, from the youngest to the oldest, bears a hand, shut in the qualmy [nauseating] rooms, where meals are cooked and clothing washed and dried besides." [27]

Sweatshops were also poorly lit. The windows were usually covered with grime—if there were windows at all. Clara Lemlich, a garment worker, wrote in the *New York Evening Journal* of November 28, 1909: "There is just one row of machines that the daylight ever gets to—that is the front row, nearest the window. The girls at all the other rows of machines back in the shops have to work by gaslight, by day as well as by night. Oh, yes, the shops keep the work going at *night,* too." [28]

Adding to the unclean atmosphere were the bathroom facilities. Toilets were usually filthy and often were located some distance away from the workers. If they were close by, the smell was awful. Workers were allowed only a few minutes' reprieve from their nonstop labor to use the facilities. Overall, sweatshops were simply dirty. Lemlich recalled, "The shops are unsanitary— that's the word that is generally used, but there ought to be a worse one used." [29]

## HOT OR COLD

Drinking water, usually warm and foul, might come only from a single tap in the hall outside. "What were you going to do?" Pauline Newman recalled. "Drink this water or none at all. Well, in those days, there were vendors who came in with bottles of pop for 2 cents, and much as you disliked to spend the two pennies you got the pop instead of the filthy water in the hall." [30]

Sweatshops could also be noisy, the machines so loud that conversation had to be kept to a minimum. Rose Cohen recalled, "The machines going at full speed drowned everything in their noise. . . . Sometimes the machines stopped for a whole minute. Then the men looked about and talked. I was always glad when the machines started off again. I felt safer in their noise." [31]

In warm weather, sweatshops literally lived up to their names. They were stiflingly hot, with little or no ventilation and nothing to create a cool breeze. In winter, the opposite was true. There was heat from a single wood or coal stove, usually the one in which the presser heated his irons, but most of the sweatshop remained bitterly cold.

Rose Cohen remembered one morning when she was especially chilled and trying to get warm. Her boss gave her three coats to work on. She spread two over her lap and hugged the third close to her body. She dared not leave her own coat on, however: "I was afraid that if he knew how cold I was he

*Women stitch garments at individual workstations in a loft building. Despite its apparent spaciousness, such large sweatshops were no more comfortable than smaller ones.*

would think I could not do as much work and would send me home and make me lose half a day's pay."[32]

## LARGER BUILDINGS

Larger sweatshops were usually located in factory buildings, also called loft buildings because of their high ceilings. Despite their greater size, loft buildings were often as uncomfortable, dark, and awkward as the small sweatshops in apartments or basements.

Sweatshop owners liked to rent the top floors of loft buildings, in part because rent was cheaper there than on the lower floors. Also, by using the increased sunlight on upper floors for lighting instead of gas jets or electricity, they could save even more money. Of course, if the windows were so covered in grime that no light got in—a common occurrence—the natural sunlight was little help.

If a sweatshop was on a high floor, employees found it was difficult just getting to work. Most of the loft buildings had staircases so narrow that only one person could ascend or descend at a time. Workers sometimes spent a full hour just getting from the street to an upper floor. Buildings equipped with elevators were not much better, since generally the elevators were inadequate for the number of people using them. It was not unusual to have only two small, slow elevators for a building with more than two thousand workers.

## LONG HOURS, SHORT BREAKS

Working days—six per week was the norm—began early and ended late. Sadie Frowne, a garment worker, wrote in 1902:

> I get up at half-past five o'clock every morning and make myself a cup of coffee on the oil stove. I eat a bit of bread and perhaps some fruit and then go to work. Often I get there soon after six o'clock so as to be in good time, though the factory does not open till seven.

> At seven o'clock we all sit down to our machines and the boss brings to each one the pile of work that he or she is to finish during the day. . . . This pile is put down beside the machine and as soon as a garment is done it is laid on the other side of the machine. Sometimes the work is not all finished by six o'clock, and then the one who is behind must work overtime. [33]

Meals were eaten in a hurry, barely pausing the work. Ruth Cohen, who worked with her father, recalled that an elderly man came by her shop daily, selling food from a basket:

> Each shop hand picked out a roll and the little old man poured him out a tiny glass of brandy for two cents. Father used to buy me an apple and a sweetened roll.

> We ate while we worked. . . . At noon we had our big meal. Then father would send me out for half a pound of steak or a slice of beef liver and a pint of beer which he sometimes bought in partnership with two or three other men. He used to broil the steak in the open coal fireplace where the presser heated his irons, and cut it into tiny squares. [34]

## TEDIUM AND COMPETITION

Adding to the dispiriting physical conditions and long hours was the sheer dullness of the work. A carpenter or other skilled craftsman could create a finished product and enjoy a job well done. No such luck for sweatshop workers, who simply repeated one small part of the project over and over—making just cuffs on sleeves, perhaps, or stems for artificial roses.

At the same time, the frantic pace of production that bosses required meant that no one could relax. Immigrant Marie Ganz recalled,

We sat in long rows, our bodies bent over the machines, the work we turned out fell into wooden bins attached to the part of the machine facing us. . . . As each girl completed her part the garment was passed on to the next girl by Levinson [the shop boss], who was always walking back and forth urging us on. Should a girl lag behind he would prod her, sometimes pulling on the garment to hurry it on to another worker.

"Hurry! Don't you see that the sleevemaker soon will have no work?" he would shout.

This sort of thing created a spirit of competition for self-preservation that ended only when the worker, too weak to compete any longer with a stronger sister, broke down.

Before many days I discovered another phase of the speed-up system. At the end of each week the girl who had turned in the least work was dropped from the payroll. Knowledge of this fact had the effect of keeping the girls working like mad. [35]

## LOW PAY

Sweatshop workers also had to deal with poor pay and erratic work schedules. Some employees were expected

*A team of women assembles shoes. The repetitive and fragmentary nature of sweatshop work provided little job satisfaction.*

## ❧ "CURSES ON HER PROUD SPIRIT" ❧

*This dialogue from a popular play of the early 1870s,* Bertha, the Sewing Machine Girl, or Death at the Wheel, *dramatizes a sweatshop worker's fight to get fair wages from her boss.*

CALEB: There, Miss Bascomb, are your wages in full, and it's more than you deserve. It is simply charity on my part. I hope that you will appreciate it.

BERTHA: Charity? Yes, it's very charitable. Very. You are charitable, Mr. Carson. Look around your factory and gaze into the faces of some of the poverty-stricken people in your employ. Contrast your ill-gotten gains with the miserable pittance paid those patient, willing hands already grown feeble with work that fills your coffers and then talk of charity. You do not know the meaning of that sacred word; not that we seek it at your hands, thank Heaven. Poor and underpaid as many of your working girls are, they inherit some of the old spirit of independence that has made our country great. And while they demand fair returns for a fair day's work, they neither ask nor will they accept from you what you call charity.

CALEB: Oho, a firebrand, eh?

BERTHA: No sir, an honest working girl, and I know of no more honorable title. (returns to her work)

CALEB: Curses on her proud spirit. I'll find some way of taming it.

to produce a certain quota of finished goods in return for fixed salaries. A more common arrangement was piecework. In this system, workers were paid according to the number of pieces completed. This created an incentive to work quickly and for long hours. Journalist Ray Stannard Baker wrote in 1904, "It was no uncommon thing . . . for men to sit bent over a sewing machine continuously from eleven to fifteen hours a day in July weather, operating a sewing machine by foot power, and often so driven that they could not stop for lunch."[36]

Whether salary or piecework, the money was never enough to cover more than bare necessities. The average wage for women in the garment industry in 1910, working a ten- to twelve-hour day, six or seven days a week, was $5 a week or $250 a year. A more experienced worker might get an annual salary of $350 to $400. Men made slightly more.

To put this in perspective, subsistence for an urban family of five in 1910 was $1,000 a year. In other words, the combined income of two experienced adults in the garment industry was still below the poverty level. Writer Françoise Basch notes, "A study of the shirtwaist worker's budget shows that [typical] wages could not possibly cover the basic outlays for food, lodging, and medical bills." [37]

## "DON'T COME IN ON MONDAY"

Related to the problem of low wages was the fact that sweatshop workers had uncertain schedules and no guarantees of future work. Even salaried workers could be fired for any number of reasons with no notice and no unemployment insurance to tide them over until another job was found. Piecework employees had even less security, never knowing from day to day if there would still be work.

Extra pay for working overtime did not exist. During the garment industry's busy spring and fall seasons, for example, workers might be expected to work sixteen hours a day, seven days a week, with no overtime. Pauline Newman recalled one sweatshop "giving us a piece of apple pie for supper instead of additional pay!" [38]

Employees who did not work overtime risked dismissal. A sign posted by the elevator at the Triangle Shirtwaist Company every Saturday during their busy season highlighted "If You Don't Come In On Sunday, Don't Come In On Monday." [39]

Furthermore, even valued workers were routinely laid off during the gar-ment industry's slow winter and summer seasons. They were thus unemployed twice a year for four to eight weeks each time. Ray Stannard Baker commented that both slow and busy times were dispiriting for workers: "The seasonal character of the work meant demoralizing toil for a few months in the year and a not less demoralizing idleness for the remainder of the time." [40]

Nor was the garment industry the only seasonal sweatshop work. Social worker Mary Van Kleeck wrote in 1913 about a New York City family that made artificial flowers:

In a tenement on MacDougal Street lives a family of seven—grandmother, father, mother and four children ages four years, three years, two years and one month respectively. All excepting the father and the two babies make violets. The three year old girl picks apart the petals; her sister, aged four years, separates the stems, dipping an end of each into paste spread on a piece of board on the kitchen table; and the mother and grandmother slip the petals up the stems.

"We all must work if we want to earn anything," said the mother.

They are paid ten cents for a gross, 144 flowers, and if they work steadily from eight or nine o'clock in the morning until 7 or 8 at night, they may make twelve gross, $1.20. In the busy season their combined earnings are usually $7.00 a week. During five months, from April to October, they have no work. [41]

## "THE SURVIVAL OF THE MEANEST"

Some sweatshop bosses and managers were no doubt humane and compassionate. However, many were not. Sweatshop workers endured frequent, even routine, mistreatment at the hands of their employers. Labor leader Meyer London commented in the 1920s, "The cloak trade at present is the trade par excellence in which the 'survival of the fittest' has come to mean 'the survival of the meanest.'" [42]

Employees were often unwilling to complain about mistreatment. They desperately needed work, and they knew that if they quit there were plenty of others waiting. If sweatshop workers wanted to stay employed, therefore, they could not afford to rock the boat. They had to be on time, do their jobs, and keep their mouths shut even in the face of unfairness, danger, or cruelty.

Bosses had many ways to take advantage of workers. One was to make workers pay for items they used. Garment workers, for instance, were often forced to buy their own thread, needles, sewing machines, and electricity. Bosses could also deduct from paychecks for the use of coat lockers or even the chairs or boxes workers sat on.

And, of course, damaged goods meant docked pay. A boss could withhold an employee's pay just by claiming that finished garments were faulty, even if it was not true. Clara Lemlich wrote, "Whenever we tear or damage any of the goods we sew on, or whenever it is found damaged after we are through with it, whether we have done it or not, we are charged for the piece and sometimes for a whole yard of the material." [43]

## MORE FINES

Bosses could fine workers for even small infractions of the rules. If an employee arrived late, for instance, she might be docked a penny for every minute she missed—even if her salary came to only fifteen cents an hour. Or, as punishment for a few minutes' tardiness, the boss might forbid her to work before lunch—thus forcing her to lose half a day's wages.

A few minutes lost at other times of the day also meant trouble. Pauline Newman recalled, "If you were two or three minutes longer [in the bathroom] than foremen or foreladies thought you should be, it was deducted from your pay. If you came five minutes late in the morning because the freight elevator didn't come down to take you up in time, you were sent home for a half a day without pay." [44]

Bosses constantly found new tactics for squeezing more work for less pay from their employees. One trick was to give workers slips of paper on which to record productivity. These were to be handed in before workers were paid. The slips were easily lost, however—in which case the worker got nothing.

Some owners cheated by altering their clocks. One garment worker testified, "I worked for the Bijou Waist Company and they made us work long hours by moving the hands of the clock when we did not see it. Sometimes we found that we got 20 minutes for lunch and that when the clock showed 5 it was really after 6." [45]

*Garment workers share cramped workspace in a dilapidated sweatshop.*

## SEXUAL HARASSMENT

Since there were no laws against it, bosses were often guilty of harassing women or of allowing male workers to harass them. Clara Lemlich commented, "The bosses in the shops are hardly what you would call educated men, and the girls to them are part of the machines they are running. They yell at the girls and they 'call them down' even worse than I imagine the Negro slaves were in the South."[46]

Female employees could sometimes handle such situations well. Rose Cohen recalled that the first sentence she learned in English was specifically taught to her so that she could deflect a boss's unwelcome advances: "Keep your hands off, please."[47] Another woman recalled quitting a job because of harassment, but not before she got revenge of a sort: "One day the machines—these old machines—broke; I had to get on the table to reach [the power belt] and the boss, an old man, he went and pinched me. So I gave him a crack and he fell. He was very embarrassed, so the whole shop went roaring [with laughter]. He thought I would keep quiet."[48]

Other small humiliations were simply part of everyday life on the job. Pauline Newman recalled "the searching of your purse or any package you happen to have lest you may have taken a bit of lace or thread."[49] Bosses expected workers to quietly put up with such abuse. Typical of the attitude was this comment from a boss: "I want no experienced girl . . . [but instead] these greenhorns [who] cannot speak English . . . and they just come from the old country, and I let them work hard, like the devil, for less wages."[50]

## SOCIALIZING

Despite its generally grim nature, life in a sweatshop was not always terrible. Some bosses forbade social interaction, arguing that it made workers less productive. However, many were more lenient. They felt that employees worked harder if they had a relaxed atmosphere. Some shops therefore allowed luxuries such as smoking and drinking on the job. According to the observer of one shop, "Most of [the workers] smoke cigarettes while they work; beer and cheap whiskey are brought in several times a day by a peddler."[51]

Radio was not widely heard until later in the century, so workers did not listen to broadcasts, but they could sing if their workplaces were not too noisy. Familiar folk melodies and popular American songs were perennial favorites. One Boston worker recalled, "We used to sing Russian songs and Yiddish songs, and the American songs, I liked very much the American songs, the 1912 songs. I loved it."[52]

Conversation also gave sweatshops an air of community. Workers who spoke English taught it to new arrivals

## ❧ "THE THINGS WHICH I COULD SEE" ❧

*Immigrant Rose Cohen, in this excerpt from her memoir* Out of the Shadow: A Russian Jewish Girlhood on the Lower East Side, *recalls her observations on her first day as a baster in a garment sweatshop:*

All afternoon I sat on my high stool, a little away from the table, my knees crossed tailor fashion, basting flaps. As I worked I watched the things which I could see by just raising my eyes a little. . . .

A big man stood at a big table, examining, brushing and folding coats. There was a window over his table through which the sun came streaming in, showing millions of specks of dust dancing over the table and circling over his head. He often puffed out his cheeks and blew the dust from him with a great gust so that I could feel his breath at our table.

or passed on the latest gossip and news. On-the-job talk could also be educational. Many workers, even if they were not formally educated, were keenly interested in intellectual topics such as philosophy, politics, the arts, or religion. Immigrant Marcus Ravage recalled,

The sweatshop was my first university. . . . When I overheard a dispute between the young buttonhole maker and the cadaverous, curly-haired closer, on the respective merits of the stories of Chekhov and Maupassant; and when, another day, the little black-eyed Russian girl who was receiving two cents per dozen shirts as a finisher boldly asserted that evolution pointed the way to anarchism and not to socialism, and cited the fact that Spencer

himself was an anarchist, my eyes were opened and I felt ashamed of my ignorance.[53]

## "IT DOESN'T MATTER"

Sweatshops certainly were not paradises, but they could sometimes be fairly congenial places in which to spend the day. Pauline Newman recalled that a convivial atmosphere sometimes made workers reluctant to move from one shop to another:

What good would it do to change jobs since similar conditions existed in all garment factories of that era? . . . One gets used to a place even if it is only a work shop. One gets to know the people you work with. You are no longer a stranger and alone. You have a feeling of belonging which helps to make life in a factory a bit easier to endure. Very often friendships are formed and a common understanding established. [54]

Another veteran of the garment trade added, "There are certain wonderful things about the industry. You don't need English; it doesn't matter what your age, what you look like, or how you dress." [55]

Nonetheless, overall sweatshop life withered the soul and tamped down individuality. At times, it was also physically dangerous.

# CHAPTER 3

# DANGERS IN THE SWEATSHOP

Illness and injury, or the threat of illness and injury, were daily events in sweatshops. In such close quarters, workers could easily contract infectious, sometimes fatal diseases such as tuberculosis, typhoid, influenza, and scarlet fever.

They could just as easily suffer physical injuries or even accidental deaths. In some sweatshops, chemical poisoning was common. And the constant threat of fire was perhaps the greatest workplace danger of all.

Such hazards were especially terrifying for sweatshop workers because no economic safety nets existed at the time. There was no such thing, for instance, as workmen's compensation, which guarantees an income for injured or ill workers. Anyone out of work for these reasons was simply out of luck.

## BREEDING GROUNDS FOR DISEASE

Sweatshops were perfect breeding grounds for a variety of contagious illnesses. Their crowded damp rooms and poor sanitation fostered disease and accelerated its spread. It was more or less impossible to keep clean in sweatshops. Besides the filthy lavatories, many shops had no sinks or washbasins. Some did not even have running water. Such conditions led easily to the spread of disease.

One observer in 1893 noted conditions found in Boston's sweatshops by the Massachusetts Bureau of Labor: Employees worked in "basements where dampness was added to cold and bad air. . . . There are no conveniences [bathrooms] for women; and men and women use the same closets, wash-basins, and drinking cups, etc. . . . In [one shop] a water-closet [toilet] in the center of

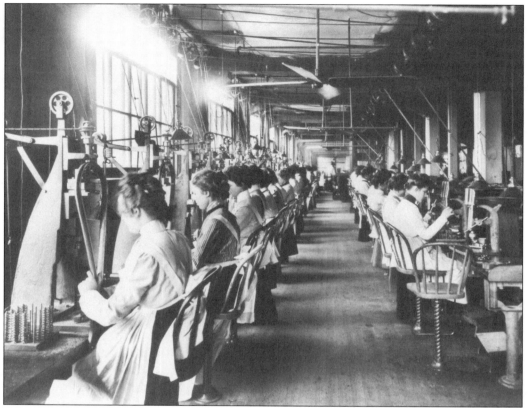

*Female machinists work in very close quarters. Crowded conditions in the sweatshop facilitated the spread of illness and disease.*

the room filled it with a sickening stench."[56]

Once picked up, disease traveled easily from the workplace to home and beyond. In sweatshops that produced consumable products such as canned food or cigars, for example, there were no requirements that workers wash their hands or avoid coughing. An infected worker could easily contaminate products.

Sometimes infectious diseases were passed on via other sorts of products.

Social reformer Florence Kelley testified in 1899 before a national committee about one case that was caught in time: "I found an overcoat, a good summer overcoat, being made up in a room in which there was a patient dying of smallpox; that was in Twentieth Street, in Chicago; and the hanger on the coat, the little silk strap, was marked with the name of a custom tailor in Helena, Montana. . . . If we had not caught it, the garment would have gone back [infected with smallpox]."[57]

## "THE TAILOR'S DISEASE"

Tuberculosis, a serious respiratory disease that at the time was a leading cause of death, was perhaps the most common contagious disease among sweatshop workers. Also called TB or consumption, tuberculosis was so prevalent in the garment trade that it was known as "the tailor's disease" or "the Jewish disease."

A social worker, Ernest Poole, wrote a report on the subject that poignantly began: "'Breath—breath—give me breath.' A Yiddish whisper, on a night in April 1903, from the heart of the New York ghetto. At 18 Clinton Street, back in the rear tenement, a young Roumanian Jew lay dying of consumption. . . .'"[58]

The disease was not restricted to just the Jewish population, of course. Dr. Antonio Stella, a physician who worked among New York City's immigrant Italians, wrote in 1917:

To have an idea of the alarming frequency of consumption among Italians, especially in the large cities, one must follow the Italian population as it moves in the tenement districts; study them closely in their daily struggle for air and space; see them in the daytime crowded in sweatshops and factories; at night heaped together in dark, windowless rooms. . . .

Six months of life in the tenements are sufficient to turn the sturdy youth from Calabria, the brawny fisherman of Sicily, the robust women from Abruzzi and Basilicata, into the pale, flabby undersized creatures we see, dragging along the streets of New York and Chicago, such a painful contrast to the native population! Six months more of this gradual deterioration, and

## ❧ THE REAL MENACE ❧

*For the average sweatshop worker, the tasks themselves were not usually seriously dangerous. Rather, danger was created by a variety of unsafe conditions, including a lack of safety mechanisms on machinery or poor ventilation. Dr. George Price, a safety inspector in New York City, noted more of these conditions in 1911. The excerpt is reprinted in Stein's* Out of the Sweatshop:

The real menace to the health of the workers and the real dangers in their lives, lie . . . not in the peculiar character of the work but in the inadequate provisions for fire protection, in the insufficient light and illumination, in the overcrowded and unventilated shops, in the lack of cleanliness, and in the absence of needed comforts and conveniences.

the soil for the bacillus tuberculosis is amply prepared.[59]

## RELATIVELY MINOR INJURIES

Physical injury was also commonplace for sweatshop workers. The twenty-five-pound hand-operated pressing irons typically used in garment sweatshops, for instance, were a common cause of spinal curvature, burns, or crushed fingers. There were few, if any, safety guards on these or other types of machinery.

Injuries were not necessarily fatal or even very serious. A typical garment shop accident, for instance, might be a finger pierced by a sewing machine needle or a burn from a hot iron. In soap factories, workers' hands were damaged by caustic soda, so that by the end of the day their fingers were raw and bleeding. When cleaning and packing fish, workers blistered their hands and fingers using a chemical called saltpeter.

Such relatively small injuries were so frequent that most workers hardly noticed them. Sadie Frowne recalled, "The machines go like mad all day because the faster you work the more money you get. Sometimes in my haste I get my finger caught and the needle goes right through it. It goes so quick, though, that it does not hurt much. I bind the finger up with a piece of cotton and go on working. We all have accidents like that."[60]

In many sweatshops, workers had to provide their own bandages or pay for them. One observer wrote about a typical shop, "For the first three times the wounds are dressed without charge. After that the person injured must pay expenses."[61]

## MORE SERIOUS INJURIES

In sweatshops with large machines, as in textile factories that produced rolls of uncut cloth, serious accidents such as boiler explosions were more common. Perhaps the most common serious injuries in these factories were sustained when ragged or loose clothing, or long hair carelessly left hanging down, got caught in large, fast-moving machines. Such accidents could easily result in an arm ripped off, scalping, or worse.

Children suffered especially high amounts of serious injury in the workplace partly because of their smaller size, short attention spans, and lower stamina. Adding to this was the fact that the cotton mills of the South used large numbers of child laborers, and the machines in these mills were especially large and dangerous. A prominent psychology professor, William O. Krohn, spoke about the problems of serious injury to children before the National Conference of Charities and Correction in 1897:

Not a day passes but some child is made a helpless cripple. These

*Large, fast-moving machines, such as this mechanical loom, were responsible for many serious sweatshop injuries.*

accidents occur after three o'clock in the afternoon.

The child that has begun his work in the morning with a reasonable degree of vigor, after working under constant pressure for several hours, at about three o'clock becomes so wearied, beyond the point of recovery, that he can no longer direct the tired fingers and aching arms with any degree of accuracy. He thus becomes the prey of the great cutting knives, or of the jaws of the tin-stamping machine.[62]

*A woman attaches soles to shoes with the help of a sewing machine. The tedious and grueling character of sweatshop work often led to depression and physical exhaustion.*

## EXHAUSTION

The health of sweatshop workers—children and adults alike—was jeopardized in other ways as well. One was when they succumbed to emotional illnesses such as depression and stress. On occasion, such illnesses could lead to feelings of hopelessness—and perhaps to desperate acts such as suicide or killing one's family to spare them a life of poverty.

Events like these were relatively rare, however. More common was an overall breakdown in health caused by sheer exhaustion. The problem of exhaustion affected all workers, but the pressure to work every possible moment was of particular danger to pregnant women. Historian Barbara Mayer Wertheimer writes, "Pregnant women stayed on the job so close to the time they delivered that babies were sometimes born right in the factory between the looms. It was work or starve."[63]

Exhaustion causing a breakdown in health was also acute among child laborers, as writer Edward Markham noted in 1907:

All the year in New York and in other cities you may watch children radiating to and from [their] pitiful homes. Nearly any hour on the East Side of New York City you can see them—pallid boy or spindling [thin] girl—their faces dulled, their backs bent under a heavy load of garments piled on head and shoulders, the muscles of the whole frame in a long strain. The boy always has bowlegs and walks with feet wide apart and wobbling.

In the rush times of the year, preparing for the changes of seasons . . . there are no idle fingers in the sweatshops. A little child of "seven times one" can be very useful in threading needles, in cutting the loose threads left on, or for any stitch broken by the little bungling fingers. The light is not good, but baby eyes must "look sharp". . . .

Is it not a cruel civilization that allows little hearts and little shoulders to strain under these grown-up responsibilities, while in the same city a pet cur [dog] is jeweled and pampered and aired on a fine lady's velvet lap on the beautiful boulevards?[64]

## FIRE HAZARDS

Fire was a danger in virtually every sweatshop in America, even those in newer buildings that were allegedly fireproof. The "fireproofing" of these newer buildings was only effective for the buildings themselves; fireproofing might protect a building's brick and

---

## ❧ A DIFFERENT KIND OF OPPRESSION ❧

*Crusading journalist Ray Stannard Baker wrote often on the poor health environments and other problems of sweatshop workers. This excerpt from "Plight of the Tailors," a 1904 magazine piece, is reprinted in Stein's* Out of the Sweatshop:

A bronzed, wiry young peasant, coming here to the land of freedom and hope from the oppressions of Russia, sat down at a sewing machine in a hot, dusty, fetid tenement-shop in East Broadway or Clinton Street; and sometimes he lasted five years, sometimes seven, rarely ten. . . .

He had merely changed oppressions—from the political tyranny of Russia to the industrial tyranny of America; and while the former had robbed him of some of his rights, the latter took his life.

steel but still easily destroy the lives and material inside it.

Garment sweatshops were especially vulnerable to fire because they were crammed with flammable hazards from ceiling to floor. Thousands of pounds of highly flammable material such as fabric scraps, cleaning solutions, and sewing machine oil were routinely stored near workers. Often this flammable material was in the same crowded rooms as the workers— or under them, since workers often sat on piles of cloth as they worked.

In addition, sewing machines leaked oil; even sewing machines that were in good repair leaked a little. These machines were often arranged in rows, and over time the wooden floors beneath them would be impregnated with oil. Despite regulations forbidding smoking in dangerous areas, the practice was commonplace—and a careless match, cigarette, or spark from a machine could quickly set this oil ablaze.

Factory owners and foremen routinely ignored regulations about smoking and other safety issues, and overworked (or corrupt) city inspectors often ignored them as well. Alfred E. Smith, then a New York State legislator and later governor, was a member of a state safety commission formed in 1911. He later recalled,

> So lax had the state been prior to 1911 . . . that there was no way for the state even to know when a factory was started. A man could hire a floor in a loft building, put in his machinery and start his factory. There was no provision of law that required him to notify the state that he was engaging in a business. . . .

Factory-inspection forces were so small that the inspections in some cities were made only once in two years and in others once a year. Factory managers knew just about when to expect an inspection, and consequently, during the day of the inspector's visit everything was in shipshape. The rest of the year it was allowed to run haphazard, there being no fear of detection by the authorities.[65]

## VIOLATIONS

Smith's commission discovered hundreds of violations in the sample of New York garment sweatshops it studied. Many shops, for instance, had defective drop ladders for fire escapes— or no fire escapes at all. Single exits and unlit hallways were commonplace. Many had doors that opened inward. These were potentially deadly because panicked workers, crushed against doors and trying to get out, would have been unable to open the doors. Most had too few, if any, sand-filled fire buckets or operable fire hoses.

## ❧ LOCKED IN ❧

*Sweatshop bosses frequently locked their workers in, justifying their actions on the grounds of preventing stealing or "protecting the workers." However, locked doors were death sentences in the event of a fire. This news bulletin from the* Daily Forward *newspaper reports on one incident that, thankfully, did not involve a fire:*

August 4, 1904—The seven cloakmakers who work at the Harris and Samuels Company, on the eighth floor of 97 Fifth Avenue, decided last night to stop work early, at 9 P.M.

But when they wanted to get out of the place, they discovered that the boss wasn't back yet to open the locked door. One of them had a key to the shop that would open the door only from the outside. So they waited some time. But the boss forgot to return.

After waiting for an hour and a half, they opened the windows and yelled down their predicament to passers-by who called the firemen who brought a ladder that was just a few inches short of the eighth floor.

Finally, one of the trapped cloakmakers remembered his key. He threw it down and one of the firemen unlocked the door.

---

Many shops were on or above the seventh floor of their buildings, farther than standard fire ladders and hoses could reach. Furthermore, the doors that led from a sweatshop to its building's staircases were often kept locked. Employers justified this practice by claiming that workers should not be "interrupted," or that locked doors cut down on theft.

Smith's commission was formed in the wake of one particular, horrifying event: a fire on March 25, 1911, at the Triangle Shirtwaist Company in New York City. This disaster, the worst catastrophe in the history of sweatshops, killed 146 people, most of them Jewish and Italian immigrant women between the ages of thirteen and twenty-three.

## THE TRIANGLE FIRE

There were about five hundred people at Triangle on the day of the fire. They occupied the top three floors of the Asch Building, a relatively new and allegedly fireproof structure. On the eighth floor the cutters, mostly men, cut pieces from large bolts of cloth. On the floor above, the seamstresses, all women, sat at 240 sewing machines, arranged in tightly packed rows with the workers sitting back to back. The tenth floor was reserved for offices, a showroom, and space for pressing and packing garments for shipping.

The blaze started on the eighth floor. The exact cause was never determined; whatever the reason, it was fed by flammable liquid and thousands of pounds of fabric. Fire spread rapidly

*Firefighters use high-pressure water cannons to extinguish the Triangle Shirtwaist fire.*

to the ninth and tenth floors, and panic immediately set in.

Those on the tenth floor escaped by climbing to the roof and over to the adjoining building. Most of the others, however, did not have an easy escape route.

They tried desperately to use the building's two staircases. One was locked, however, and a crush of people soon jammed the other. The outside fire escape, overloaded with people, soon collapsed.

The building's two elevator operators worked their elevators as quickly as possible, but it was not enough for the crush of panicked people. Some of the women on the ninth floor, desperate to get out, pried open the elevator doors and threw themselves down the shafts. Passengers inside the cars later reported hearing the thud of bodies on top of the cars, then the rattling of coins as they fell out of the women's pockets.

## "A HORRIFYING SPECTACLE"

The fire spread rapidly, engulfing the building's upper floors. Many workers, suffocating and trapped inside the burning rooms, had no other choice but to leap to the street below. Some who fell already were engulfed in flames, their clothes burning. By the time the fire department arrived, the litter of bodies on the street was so thick that it slowed the fire trucks down. Then it was discovered that the fire ladders were only long enough to reach the sixth floor—not enough to be useful.

Passersby and firemen tried to catch some of the jumping women with stretched-out safety nets, blankets, even jackets. Such efforts were of little use, and dead bodies lay everywhere. William Shepherd, a newspaper reporter, wrote in an eyewitness account, "The floods of water from the firemen's hose that ran into the gutter were actually stained red with blood." [66]

Frances Perkins, later a prominent workplace safety investigator and U.S. secretary of labor, was by coincidence a witness to the disaster. She recalled:

I happened to have been visiting a friend on the other side of the park and we heard the engines and we heard the screams and . . . rushed over where we could see what the trouble was. We could see this building from Washington Square and the people had just begun to jump when we got there.

They had been holding [on] until that time, standing in the windowsills, being crowded by others behind them, the fire pressing closer and closer, the smoke closer and closer. Finally . . . they couldn't wait any longer.

They began to jump. The window was too crowded and they would jump and they hit the sidewalk. The net broke, they [fell] a terrible distance, the weight of the bodies was so great, at the speed at which they were traveling . . . they broke through the net. Every one of them was killed, everybody who jumped was killed. It was a horrifying spectacle. [67]

## OUT OF TRAGEDY, CHANGE

The fire shocked New York City and horrified the entire country. Newspaper reports began to examine not only the fire prevention deficiencies of the Triangle Building but those of other buildings and sweatshops. As the full extent of the dangers became clearer to the American public, they grew increasingly shocked and angered.

The Triangle disaster served as a central symbol for this outrage. It stood for everything that was wrong with the sweatshop system, and it became a rallying point for reform-minded people who hoped to make things better for sweatshop workers. In many ways, some historians feel, the Triangle fire was the single most important event—good or bad—in the history of sweatshops and the lives of sweatshop workers.

Some good did come out of the tragedy. As a direct result of the fire, a number of significant safety laws were

*An inspector indicates a door of the Triangle Shirtwaist factory in the aftermath of the fire. Kept locked to prevent theft, the factory doors provided no escape from the flames.*

passed around the country. A plaque on the present site of the Asch Building referring to the fire's victims makes this connection clear. It states, "Out of their martyrdom came new concepts of social responsibility and labor legislation that have helped make American working conditions the finest in the world."[68]

Nowhere was the aftermath of the Triangle disaster more keenly felt than in the slums where the victims and their families had lived. These slums were often as grim and as dangerous as the sweatshops themselves. Nonetheless, the lives of workers outside the sweatshops could contain elements of pleasure, satisfaction, and even joy.

# CHAPTER 4

# LIFE OUTSIDE THE SWEATSHOP

Once their long day of labor was over, sweatshop workers headed home. They lived in crowded, crumbling apartments called tenements—buildings that were just as dispiriting as the sweatshops in which they spent most of their waking hours.

Usually, there was just enough time to catch a few hours of sleep before starting a new cycle of work. However, even the dreariest life could be lightened with moments of recreation. Fancy theaters, high-class restaurants, and exclusive stores may have been beyond the means of sweatshop workers, but they managed nonetheless to find some pleasure.

One young garment worker, Sadie Frowne, summed up this attitude in a 1902 newspaper article: "The machines are all run by foot power, and at the end of the day one feels so weak that there is a great temptation to lie right down and sleep. But you must go out and get air, and have some pleasure. So instead of lying down I go out, generally with Henry.

"I am very fond of dancing and, in fact, all sorts of pleasure. I go to the theatre quite often, and like those plays that make you cry a great deal." [69]

## TENEMENTS

Virtually all sweatshop workers—and every other poor urban dweller—lived in tenements. As one little girl poignantly stated, her tenement home was "a place so dark it seemed as if there weren't no sky." [70] A typical tenement building was five or six stories high, each floor holding about fourteen rooms. Only a few rooms on each floor received sunlight and fresh air; most were dark and windowless, lit only by gas jets or candles. Often, only a single outside toilet served everyone who lived in the building, and some individual apartments had no sinks, tubs, or hot water.

*Rows of laundry hang to dry above the yard of a New York City tenement complex.*

Developers did not have to follow strict safety codes, and landlords had no obligations to maintain buildings, so tenements deteriorated quickly. A committee of architects in Boston inspecting typical buildings in 1899 reported on their conditions: "Dirty and battered walls and ceilings, dark cellars with water standing in them, alleys littered with garbage and filth, broken and leaking drain-pipes . . . dark and filthy water-closets [toilets], closets long frozen or otherwise out of order . . . and houses so dilapidated and so much settled [on their foundations] that they are dangerous." [71]

In winter, heat was uncertain and dependent on the whims of the landlord, and there was no such thing as air-conditioning in the sweltering heat of summer. Tenement dwellers naturally sought refuge from the summer heat outside, on roofs, fire escapes, and sidewalks. Jacob Riis noted,

It is in hot weather, when life indoors is well-nigh unbearable with cooking, sleeping, and working, all crowded into the small rooms together, that the tenement expands, reckless of all restraint. Then a strange and picturesque life moves upon the flat roofs. In the day and early evening mothers air their babies there, the boys fly their kites from the house-tops, undismayed by police regulations, and the young men and girls court and pass the growler [beer bucket]. [72]

## "ONLY MILLIONAIRES CAN BE ALONE"

Tenements were always crowded to the bursting point. Struggling families often let relatives or boarders share rooms to help with the rent, and landlords were eager to crowd as many

---

## ᴄ᷉ A VISIT TO THE TENEMENT ᷉ᴅ

*This passage from Jacob Riis's* How the Other Half Lives *vividly describes a typical tenement scene. The "soiled bow of white" is a sign of mourning:*

Be a little careful, please! The hall is dark and you might stumble over the children pitching pennies back there. Not that it would hurt them; kicks and cuffs are their daily diet. They have little else. Here where the hall turns and dives into utter darkness is a step, and another, another. A flight of stairs. You can feel your way, if you cannot see it.

Close? Yes! What would you have? All the fresh air that ever enters these stairs comes from the hall-door that is forever slamming, and from the windows of dark bedrooms that in turn receive from the stairs their sole supply of the elements God meant to be free, but man deals out with such niggardly [stingy] hand.

That was a woman filling her pail by the hydrant you just bumped against. The sinks are in the hallway, that all the tenants may have access—and all be poisoned alike by their summer stenches. Hear the pump squeak! It is the lullaby of tenement-house babes. In summer, when a thousand thirsty throats pant for a cooling drink in this block, it is worked in vain.

But the saloon, whose open door you passed in the hall, is always there. The smell of it has followed you up. Here is a door. Listen! That short hacking cough, that tiny, helpless wail—what do they mean? They mean that the soiled bow of white you saw on the door downstairs will have another story to tell—Oh! a sadly familiar story—before the day is at an end. The child is dying with measles. With half a chance it might have lived; but it had none. That dark bedroom killed it.

"It was took all of a suddint," says the mother, smoothing the throbbing little body with trembling hands. There is no unkindness in the rough voice of the man in the jumper, who sits by the window grimly smoking a clay pipe, with the little life ebbing out in his sight, bitter as his words sound: "Hush, Mary! If we cannot keep the baby, need we complain—such as we?"

paying tenants in as possible. As a result, there was little hope of privacy for the poor. A sweatshop worker in Anzia Yezierska's novel *The Bread Givers* wryly observed, "Only millionaires can be alone in America."[73]

It was not uncommon for half a dozen people to live in one small room, or for a hundred people to live in a building originally meant to accommodate a few families. The *Jewish Forward* newspaper illustrated what happens with such overcrowding when it reported in 1905 the findings of an investigator for a maternity hospital:

166 Norfolk Street. The happy parents welcome their first child. They live in a furnished room, together with two other couples. There is only one bed. When the doctor asks where they sleep, they can only reply that they manage somehow. The doctor thinks they take turns, each night a different couple uses the bed. Or perhaps

*This Jacob Riis photo shows more than six tenement dwellers sharing a living space no larger than a modern bathroom.*

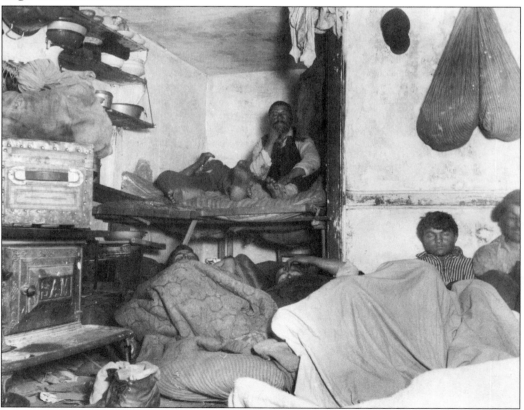

on an hourly schedule: One couple has the bed till midnight, then it goes to the other.[74]

Single women generally lived in boardinghouses, which supplied room and board and were usually run by older women who acted as surrogate mothers. Single men often lived in less fancy flophouses, where they could rent a hammock or space on the floor for a few pennies a night.

The cheapest flophouses did not even supply horizontal sleeping space. For a penny a night in these places, men hung by their armpits on a clothesline strung across a room. Jacob Riis wryly commented, "In the morning the boss [landlord] woke them up by simply untying the line at one end and letting it go with its load; a labor-saving device certainly, and highly successful in attaining the desired end."[75]

## HEALTH CONCERNS

As in the sweatshops where they worked, overcrowded and unclean tenements created serious health hazards for sweatshop workers and their families. Disease and malnutrition were common and widespread problems. The death rates for immigrants, children and adults alike, were much higher than were those for native-born Americans who lived outside the tenements.

Epidemics of such diseases as influenza, typhoid, smallpox, tuberculosis, and cholera regularly attacked the slums. In those days, antibiotics and other lifesaving medicines had not yet been discovered. As a result, many diseases that are today easily treatable (or are completely eradicated) caused widespread death.

Typical was a measles epidemic that devastated three crowded New York City blocks, killing as many as eight children in a single house. Jacob Riis wrote, "When it had spent its fury, the death-maps in the Bureau of Vital Statistics looked as if a black hand had been laid across those blocks. . . . The track of the epidemic through these teeming barracks was as clearly defined as the track of a tornado through a forest district."[76]

Compounding the problem was the fact that there was no such thing as health insurance in those days. People who lived from paycheck to paycheck could rarely afford the added expense of a doctor's visit or a bottle of medicine. They often relied, with varying degrees of success, on folk remedies brought from the old country, such as chicken soup and mustard plasters for colds.

Charity hospitals—the only sort available to most poor workers—often were of little help. In some ways, these hospitals could be more harmful than helpful and were often avoided by poor sweatshop workers. Patients in charity hospitals often had to share beds, sterilization was minimal, and— since hospital staff often tried to avoid

# ❧ AT HOME ☙

*Future union organizer Pauline Newman reminisces here, in a passage reprinted in Barbara Mayer Wertheimer's* We Were There: The Story of Working Women in America, *on her tenement life:*

You got out of the workshop, dark and cold in winter, hot in summer, dirty unswept floors, no ventilation, and you would go home. What kind of home did you go to? You won't find the ten-ements [now that] we lived in. Some of the rooms didn't have any windows. I lived in a two-room tenement with my mother and two sisters and the bedroom had no windows, the facilities [toilets] were down in the yard, but that's the way it was in the factories too. In the summer the sidewalk, fire escapes, and the roof of the tenements became bedrooms just to get a breath of air.

*A family of eight pauses from the day's labors to enjoy a simple meal.*

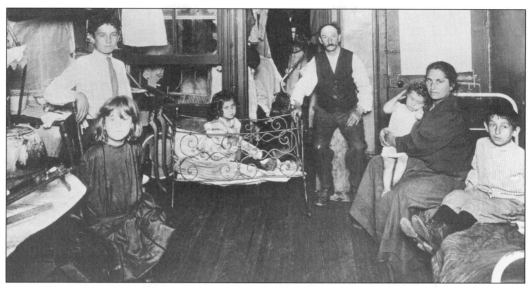

*A family poses amid their meager possessions in their tiny tenement home.*

touching patients—sick people frequently went unwashed for long periods.

## FRUGALITY

It was important for sweatshop workers to save every penny they made, especially since many sent money back to relatives in Europe. Workers therefore had to be frugal in every way. Shirtwaist maker and union organizer Pauline Newman recalled, "We wore cheap clothes, lived in cheap tenements, ate cheap food."[77]

Somehow, though, even large families got by. Journalist Zalman Yoffeh recalled of his tenement childhood,

> With one dollar a day [our mother] fed and clothed an ever-growing family. She took in boarders.

Sometimes this helped; at other times it added to the burden of living. Boarders were often out of work and penniless; how could one turn a hungry man out?

> She made all our clothes. She walked blocks to reach a place where meat was a penny cheaper, where bread was a half cent less. She collected boxes and old wood to burn in the stove instead of costly coal. Her hands became hardened and the lines so begrimed that for years she never had perfectly clean hands.

> One by one she lost her teeth—there was no money for dentists—and her cheeks caved in. Yet we children always had clean

## ❧ TWO CENTS WIN THE DAY ❧

*Jacob Riis, in* How the Other Half Lives, *describes the typical evening meal—the one "square meal" of the day—that sweatshop workers on the Lower East Side of New York were accustomed to:*

I know of a couple of restaurants at the lower end of Orchard Street that are favorite resorts for the Polish Jews. . . . Being neighbors, they are rivals of course, and cutting under [undercutting prices]. When I was last there one gave a dinner of soup, meat-stew, bread, pie, pickles, and a "schooner" of beer for thirteen cents; the other charged fifteen cents for a similar dinner, but with two schooners of beer and a cigar, or a cigarette, as the extra inducement. The two cents had won the day, however, and the thirteen-cent restaurant did such a thriving business that it was about to spread out into the adjoining store to accommodate the crowds of customers.

and whole clothing. There was always bread and butter in the house, and, wonder of wonders, there was usually a penny apiece for us to buy candy with. [78]

## STYLISHNESS

Money always had to be carefully rationed by single people as well as families. Historian Moses Rischin wrote, "Bread at two and three cents a pound, milk at four cents a quart, a herring for a penny or two, and apples at from one to five for a cent, depending on quality. . . . Accustomed to a slim diet, an immigrant could save much even with meager earnings and still treat himself to a bracing three-course Sabbath dinner (for fifteen cents)." [79]

Still, if pennies were carefully saved, single men and women could usually afford a little beyond the necessities. A young woman might buy a theater ticket at the end of the week, or pay for dancing lessons; a young man might save up for a book or attend a movie. Some chose to spend their spare cash on clothes. Sadie Frowne wrote in 1902,

Some of the women blame me very much because I spend so much money on clothes. They say that instead of $1 a week I ought not to spend more than 25 cents a week on clothes, and that I should save the rest.

But a girl must have clothes if she is to go into high society at [amusement parks like] Ulmer Park or Coney Island or the theatre. . . . A girl who does not dress well is stuck in a comer, even if she is pretty and Aunt Fanny says that I do just right to put on plenty of style. [80]

Many other women were willing to sacrifice for a bit of such style. Labor leader Clara Lemlich wrote in 1909, "We're human, all of us girls, and we're young. We like new hats as well as any other young women. Why shouldn't we? And if one of us gets a new one, even if it hasn't cost more than 50 cents, that means that we have gone for weeks on two-cent lunches—dry cake and nothing else." [81]

## A LIVELY STREET SCENE

Tenement neighborhoods existed in many cities, but New York had the largest and most intense concentration of tenements. The density of its Lower East Side—seven hundred people per acre, as many as four thousand in a single block—made it the most crowded neighborhood in the city and probably in the country.

Intense crowding and the desire to escape cramped apartments had a positive aspect, however: it created a lively street scene. The Lower East Side, for example, became a colorful community that recreated, as closely as possible,

*A street on New York's Lower East Side bustles with activity. The store sign in Yiddish reveals the large number of Jewish immigrants in the neighborhood.*

a typical Eastern European Jewish village. One observer marveled, "The vast east side is scarcely New York. It is Europe,—with a touch of Asia."[82]

The streets, shops, and restaurants of tenement neighborhoods were a lively jumble of activity—sometimes dangerous, sometimes dirty, but always as vivid as a stage show. A constant show was provided by the passing parade of horse-drawn carts, loud salesmen, friendly arguments between friends or unfriendly fights between enemies.

One young garment worker on the Lower East Side remarked to an interviewer that she did not even need to participate to enjoy this show. For her, simply observing was enough: "I don't like the place I live in very much, but it is great to be free to do what I want. There are so many new things to see and so much happening on the streets. I can be happy for hours, leaning out the window watching it."[83]

Sometimes the immediate neighborhood made up the whole world of an immigrant sweatshop worker. In her autobiography, social worker Jane Addams wrote,

An Italian woman once expressed her pleasure in the red roses that she saw at one of our receptions in surprise that they had been "brought so fresh all the way from Italy." She would not believe for an instant that they had been grown in America.

She said that she had lived in Chicago for six years and had never seen any roses, whereas in Italy she had seen them every summer in great profusion. During all that time, of course, the woman had lived within ten blocks of a florist's window; she had not been more than a five-cent car ride away from the public parks; but she had never dreamed of faring forth for herself, and no one had taken her. Her conception of America had been the untidy street in which she lived.[84]

## THE GAMES CHILDREN PLAYED

For tenement children, the street was the main playground. Rose Cohen recalled that when she first arrived she watched other kids before she found the courage to join them: "Our room was a dingy place where the sun never came in. I always felt lonely and a little homesick on coming into it. But I would soon shake off the feeling. I would cook and eat some soup and then go and stand on the stoop and watch the children playing."[85]

Games that required no expensive equipment, and which were easily played in a street or a vacant lot, were popular. Perennial favorites with boys were baseball, football, and stickball. A favorite game with girls, meanwhile,

*Tenement children play in the gutter water of a street on New York's Lower East Side.*

was "potsy," which was similar to hop-scotch.

Tenement dweller Samuel Chotznikoff recalled of his boyhood that it was rich and varied and involved much more than just playing games:

The days in summer and winter were crowded with incidents, amusing, soul-satisfying, perilous, or adventurous. . . . There were gang wars to be fought, policemen to annoy and outwit, and sentimental couples to be teased and ridiculed. . . .

There were ambulances to be run after and horsecars to hang on to—unobserved by the conduc-tor. If one was on intimate terms with a currier [horse attendant] in a livery stable, one could sit bareback astride a horse and ride through the streets. [86]

## "YOU BASEBALL PLAYER YOU!"

For adult residents of the tenements, there were many diversions as well. Sporting events such as boxing and baseball were favorites. Participant sports such as baseball were also very popular. Not all tenement dwellers appreciated active sports, however. Many deeply religious and intellectual Jews, for instance, disdained them and did not want their children playing them. They preferred board games such as chess, which to them indicated mental achievement over "simple" athletics. The famous entertainer Eddie Cantor, who was raised by his grandmother in New York's Lower East Side, recalled this childhood scene: "'Stop! You—you—you baseball player you!' scolded grandma, hurrying after us into the hall. That was the worst name she could call me. To the pious people of the ghetto a baseball player was the king of loafers."[87]

Gambling and drinking were also popular among some adults. Needless to say, alcohol abuse created some serious problems. Jacob Riis wrote in 1890, "Forty percent of the distress among the poor, said a recent official report, is due to drunkenness."[88] He added wryly that drinking was not always restricted to adults: "The law prohibiting the selling of beer to minors is about as much respected in the tenement-house districts as the ordinance against swearing."[89]

## LOVE AND COURTSHIP

As they always have, young men and women frequently used their free time to court one another. In many European cultures, strict rules had once governed how this could happen—only while supervised, generally, and perhaps at the woman's family home.

In America, however, a looser atmosphere often prevailed, and young people were frequently allowed out on their own. Sweatshop worker Ruth Hirsh, who came from Russia as a young girl and lived with an aunt in Pittsburgh, recalled, "I met my husband after I was a year here. . . . We used to go out, the four of us, my sister and I, and my brother and him. . . . Who was chaperoned? Not in this country."[90]

Dancing was hugely popular among single people, and tenement neighborhoods such as the Lower East Side boasted many dance halls and schools where one could learn fancy steps. Movies, vaudeville houses, live theaters, and amusement parks were also favorite pastimes for adults both young and old.

Movies were especially popular, since one could while away an entire afternoon or evening in a movie theater for a minimum of money. The *Jewish Forward* noted in 1908, "Five cents is little to pay. A movie show lasts half an hour. If it's not too busy, you can see it several times."[91]

## THE LIFE OF THE MIND

Some sweatshop workers preferred to use their free time to improve their minds. This was especially true among older Jewish immigrants, who always placed a strong emphasis on education. Writers Irving Howe and Kenneth Libo

##   &#x2767; ON TO THE DANCE &#x2766;

*In this excerpt from* Yekl *by the Yiddish novelist Abraham Cahan, the title character, a sweatshop worker, has just eaten dinner and is heading to a dance academy along the streets of the Lower East Side:*

He had to pick and nudge his way through dense swarms of bedraggled half-naked humanity; past garbage barrels rearing their overflowing contents in sickening piles, and lining the streets in malicious suggestion of rows of trees; underneath tiers and tiers of fire escapes, barricaded and festooned with mattresses, pillows, and featherbeds not yet gathered in for the night. The pent-in sultry atmosphere was laden with nausea and pierced with a discordant and, as it were, plaintive buzz. Supper had been despatched in a hurry, and the teeming populations of the cyclopic tenement houses were out in full force

"for fresh air," as even these people will say in mental quotation marks.

Suffolk Street is in the very thick of the battle for breath. For it lies in the heart of that part of the East Side which has within the last two or three decades become the Ghetto of the American metropolis, and, indeed, the metropolis of the Ghettos of the world. It is one of the most densely populated spots on the face of the earth—a seething human sea fed by streams, streamlets, and rills of immigration flowing from all the Yiddish-speaking centers of Europe. . . . Jewish runaways from justice; Jewish refugees from crying political and economical injustice; people torn from a hard-gained foothold in life and from deep-rooted attachments by the caprice of intolerance or the wiles of demagoguery . . . artisans, merchants, teachers, rabbis, artists, beggars—all come in search of fortune.

---

note, "In thousands of Yiddish-speaking homes the word *lernin* (to learn) was spoken with tones of reverence."[92]

People rarely met in their cramped homes to discuss or learn about politics or the arts, however. Those who wanted to talk about such subjects frequently used cafés, candy stores, restaurants, and pastry shops as meeting places. Certain shops and restaurants also served as informal lodges—as meeting places for immigrants from

particular towns. Natives of Vilna, for instance, might have a designated meeting spot, and those from Minsk might have another.

In the days before television and radio attending lectures was an especially popular way to learn. Immigrant Marcus Ravage recalled,

There were scores of lectures every week, I found, and I went to as many as I could. One night it was

Darwin and the next it might be the principles of air pressure. On Saturday night there were sometimes two meetings so arranged that both could be attended by the same audience. . . .

It did not matter to us what the subject was. There was a peculiar, intoxicating joy in just sitting there and drinking the words of the speakers, which to us were echoes from a higher world than ours. . . . Never in all my experience since, though I have been in college and learned societies, have I seen such earnest, responsive audiences as were those collarless men and hatless girls of the sweatshops. [93]

## "Read and Think"

Newspaper and magazine writers whose audiences were primarily sweatshop workers encouraged such forms of self-education. Typical was this comment in *The Capmakers' Journal:* "The long evenings have arrived, and it behooves all intelligent workmen to

*Many sweatshop workers used their free time to educate themselves. Here, workers of all ages learn together in a one-room school.*

spend their leisure time in equipping themselves mentally for the life task before them. Standing on the corners, playing cards, or drinking in the saloons does not tend to develop one's moral and mental makeup. But education does. Therefore, read and think."[94]

For many sweatshop workers, one aspect of the general emphasis on self-education had a direct effect on their working lives. Many discovered that educating themselves about the relationship between labor and management—that is, between themselves and their bosses—could lead to improvements in their lives. This exciting development was one aspect of the rise of the organized labor movement.

# CHAPTER 5

# THE ROLE OF ORGANIZED LABOR

Sweatshop workers were often unable to improve their working lives except in very small ways. They had little power, politically or otherwise. However, gradually and with much turmoil, the life of the average sweatshop employee began to change for the better. The primary force behind this change was the organized labor movement.

Organized labor unions—also called trade unions or simply unions—were (as they still are) groups of workers who joined together for a common cause. As a group, they fought for such basic workplace rights as higher wages, safer conditions, and shorter hours. In this way organized labor dramatically improved the lives of thousands of sweatshop workers who had previously been anonymous and powerless. As Harry Gladstone, a teenage machine tender in a sweatshop, put it to a reporter in 1898, "If you don't look out for yourself, who will? . . . The only way to get

the bosses to pay us good wages is to stick together, so let us be true to our union." [95]

## UNITED

Unions had power because they allowed ordinary workers to gain strength as a unified group. One sweatshop worker protesting against unfair practices had little power. The situation was different, however, if all the workers in a shop banded together, or if all the workers in an industry did the same. In such cases workers could negotiate with the management of companies to get what they wanted. Their power lay in the fact that if these talks were not satisfactory, the unions could strike—that is, walk out of the workplace and stop or slow its production.

Many sweatshop workers recognized that they alone were responsible for achieving their goals of decent pay and safety. Rose Schneiderman, a labor leader in the garment industry, echoed this feeling when she spoke at a memorial service shortly after the Triangle fire:

> Every week I must learn of the untimely death of one of my sister workers. Every year thousands of us are maimed. The life of men and women is so cheap and property is so sacred. . . .
>
> Too much blood has been spilled. I know from my experience it is up to the working people to save themselves. The only way they can save themselves is by a strong working-class movement.[96]

## "THE THING MOST NEEDED WAS MONEY"

Trade unions representing a variety of jobs had existed in America and Europe long before the rise of sweatshops, with varying degrees of success. Bitter fights had already been waged over "closed" shops (which hired only union members) or "open" shops (which did not).

*Sweatshop workers formed unions to obtain workplace rights. This photo depicts members of a garment workers' union striking for better pay.*

However, for several reasons union organizing in the largest group of sweatshops, the garment industry, was difficult. These shops were small and decentralized, with rapid changes in personnel and little in terms of bulky equipment or overhead; shop bosses could thus easily move their operations or simply hire new workers if trouble was brewing.

Nonetheless, sweatshop workers continued to try to organize themselves, and as the movement gained ground many employees became passionately pro-union. One sixteen-year-old Russian female garment worker, identified only as "B.A.," was typical of these enthusiastic union boosters. She told a reporter in 1913, "I think the union is like a mother and father to the children. I'd give my whole life for the union." [97]

Union supporters put everything they had into the cause. They worked long hours to foster union activity, refused to deal with any companies that were being struck, and spent hours persuading friends and coworkers to join the cause. One example of this devotion came at a meeting in 1890 that led to a garment worker's strike. One observer recalled:

The enthusiasm was indescribable. Men and women jumped on the tables. Their voices could be heard ten blocks away. After the audience cooled off a little, the chairman declared that though everybody voted for the continuation of the strike, the thing most needed was money and that was lacking, and he advised the people to reconsider their decision.

But he had hardly concluded his sentence, when one of the people walked up to the chairman's table and taking off a ring from his finger handed it over to the chairman with the request to sell it or pawn it and give the money to the strikers. In less time than it takes to tell it, the chairman's table became covered with rings, watches, ear-rings, brooches, and other pieces of jewelry. All were shouting that these offerings be sold and the strike go on. [98]

## MULTIETHNIC

Union membership came from a variety of ethnic backgrounds, reflected in the wide range of foreign language, pro-union newspapers and magazines that were published during that time. Periodicals with titles like *The Labor Standard, The Workingman's Advocate,* and *The National Labor Tribune* kept their readers informed about new developments in union activity.

Typically, the leadership of sweatshop-based unions was predominantly

## ❧ "THE BEST SORT OF A TIME" ❧

*In this passage reprinted in Wertheimer's* We Were There, *labor organizer Helen Marot describes a typical street meeting to drum up support:*

We had the best sort of a time at them. You don't have to send out notices. You just take a platform along, put up a banner and begin to talk. While someone is speaking others go round and distribute circulars among the girls and ask questions. These circulars are in Yiddish,

Italian and English and we vary them. The last one we got was on getting married. . . .

We [also] talk to the scabs when they come out [of the factories]. . . . It gives tremendous courage to the union girls to have us talk there. . . . I think these street meetings are something we can all get courage out of. We make great friends with the policemen in New York. Miss O'Reilly has already converted one policeman.

Jewish. One reason is that many of the Jewish labor leaders had come to America already experienced in political and union organizing in their native countries. However, the unions were by no means exclusively Jewish. Although at first resistant to organizing, Italian workers became an important force in garment unions, especially after many Italian women died in the Triangle fire.

Many other ethnic groups also were active in the union movement. For example, a coalition of Irish, Italian, Polish, Lithuanian, Greek, Syrian, Armenian, and Portuguese workers banded together to start a major textile strike in Lawrence, Massachusetts, in 1912. Four years later, Polish women formed the core group in a major strike against Detroit, Michigan, cigar makers.

## BLACKLISTS AND SECURITY DEPOSITS

No matter the ethnic background, some sweatshop workers were uninterested in unions. Many were afraid of the unions, believing they could lose their jobs if they joined. This was a genuine concern. Company owners were deeply threatened by the rise of the unions and bitterly opposed them. In the bosses' opinion, they themselves were the only ones who should be allowed to make decisions about wages, conditions, or hours.

They made no bones about their feelings toward union members who said otherwise. Garment worker Rose Cohen recalled one boss's reaction to an organizer: "'I'll not have any one coming into my shop and telling me what to do,' he shouted to a strange man who came over to his table to talk to him.

'This shop is mine. The machines are mine. If they are willing to work on my conditions, well and good, if not, let them go to the devil! All the tailors are not dead yet.'" [99]

Most company officials did their best to destroy, or at least hinder, union organizing. One of their milder activities was to circulate among themselves blacklists—lists of known "troublemakers." Exchanging these blacklists ensured that the people on them stayed unemployed.

Management also used other forms of intimidation. The *Jewish Forward* reported in 1904 about a "new trick of the cloak bosses who ask 'security' from the cloakmakers."

In the better shops, a worker must now deposit a $50 cash guaranty that he will neither belong to a union nor try to organize the shop, nor even dare protest against wages or working conditions.

If a cloakmaker does any of the above listed things, he not only loses his job but also forfeits his $50 deposit. In some shops a $25 deposit will do. In the cheaper line a $10 "security" is accepted. The sad fact about all this is that many cloakmakers are only too willing to deposit "security" in order to get a chance to slave for starvation wages. [100]

## VIOLENCE

Company owners also had more serious weapons at their disposal. They could hire temporary, non union workers who were willing to cross picket lines. Pro-union sweatshop workers called these much hated temporary workers "scabs."

Owners could also react with violence. Sometimes they hired strikebreakers and armed guards to intimidate, beat up, or even shoot strikers. Jacob Heller, a labor activist, recalled one especially bloody strike in 1907: "Not a day passed without numerous strikers being beaten up severely.

"Strike headquarters took on the appearance of a hospital. Bandages were evident wherever one turned. The gangsters used two methods of attack: either slashing with knives, or splitting strikers' heads with blackjacks." [101]

Some union activists, meanwhile, were prone to violence themselves. One famous episode occurred in 1886 in Chicago's Haymarket Square, where a meeting was being held to support workers lobbying for an eight-hour day. When police tried to break up the meeting, someone threw a bomb and a riot broke out. Eight police officers and one civilian died, and at least sixty people were injured, in the Haymarket Square riot.

## GOVERNMENT INTERVENTION

Police were called in to maintain order during many such tense or violent conflicts. Almost every time, the police officers were instructed by authorities to operate on the side of management. One officer candidly told a garment industry striker during a 1909 strike, "We ain't here to protect the strikers nor anybody belongin' to 'em. We're here to protect the scabs."[102]

In many cases government authorities were especially worried about the interest many workers had in socialism and communism. These political

*A union of female garment workers poses for a photo during a strike. The women in the center hold a negligee on which they have written their demands.*

theories argued that capitalism was wrong, that property and income should be evenly distributed, and that "the means of production" (such as factories) should be controlled by the people, not individuals. More radical workers, meanwhile, advocated anarchism, the complete absence of governmental restrictions.

As a result of these concerns on the part of authorities, many states passed laws during this period that were designed to restrict unions and allow businesses to operate without interference. The federal government also tightened immigration policies specifically to exclude activists and political radicals. One of these laws, President Theodore Roosevelt declared in 1903, would "exclude absolutely not only all persons who are known to be believers in anarchistic principles . . . but also all persons who are of a low moral tendency or of unsavory reputation."[103]

## "I AM A WORKING GIRL"

As the labor movement coalesced, a number of sweatshop-related unions formed and dissolved, and a series of small, more or less spontaneous strikes took place in the garment industry. These strikes were scattered, unorganized, and only moderately successful in gaining permanent, widespread change. For the average sweatshop worker, it was a confusing and unsettling time.

However, a turning point came late in 1909. That year, the Women's Trade Union League (WTUL), the first national association dedicated to organizing women workers, helped launch a large and well-organized strike against the garment industry in New York City. The garment workers who went out on strike were asking for, among other things, a 54-hour workweek, pay for overtime work, an end to unfair fines, safer workplaces, and union recognition for women workers.

A series of impassioned and heated discussions led up to the strike. At a climactic mass meeting, a fiery teenage labor leader, Clara Lemlich, interrupted one of the main speakers to make an impromptu and now famous speech. Lemlich was already a heroine to many because she had recently been badly beaten by anti-union thugs and arrested multiple times for union activities.

Speaking in Yiddish, Lemlich exclaimed: "I am a working girl, one of those striking against intolerable conditions. I am tired of listening to speakers who talk in generalities. What we are here for is to decide whether or not to strike. I offer a resolution that a general strike be declared—now." Union leaders had not meant to include a strike vote in the meeting. However, electrified by Lemlich's passionate words, the crowd overwhelmingly voted to strike against a number of major garment companies. They then joined the meeting's chairman in reciting an ancient Jewish oath of faith, repeating after him: "If I turn traitor to

## ৶ GENERAL STRIKE DECLARED TODAY 2:00PM ৡ

*This call to arms for the general garment strike of 1910 was printed on widely distributed handbills in English, Yiddish, and Italian. It is reprinted in Stein's* Out of the Sweatshop:

Today, at 2 P.M.—not earlier, not later—every cloak and skirt worker—operator, tailor, finisher, cutter, skirtmaker, presser, buttonhole maker—must put aside his work and together with all other workers go out on strike. Not one of you must remain in the shops! All out!

In leaving your shops be careful to maintain absolute order. Don't lose your heads; keep cool.

At exactly 2 P.M. each of you must pack your tools. Take them with you. Do not leave shears, shuttles or any other tools in the shops.

Leave quietly. Be orderly.

If your bosses refuse to let you use the elevators do not argue. This time, swallow your pride and descend by the stairs.

March in order from your shops to the indicated meeting halls.

Don't wait for committees to come to take you down. We will positively send no committees. We will not give the police the opportunity of making scores of arrests on this first day so that the newspapers can put out extras screaming with their headlines that our strike started with riots.

Go down yourselves.

REMEMBER: The success of the strike depends first of all on the order and discipline you show.

WE URGE AGAIN: Don't lose your heads. Maintain order and discipline.

By order of the General Strike Committee of the Cloak and Skirtmakers Union of New York International Ladies' Garment Workers' Union.

---

the cause I now pledge, may this hand wither from the arm I raise!"[104]

## THE STRIKE BEGINS

Fliers announcing the strike vote and urging garment workers to walk off the job were widely distributed in the next few days. They were written in Yiddish, Italian, and English to reach as many potential strikers as possible.

In her introduction to Theresa S. Malkiel's autobiographical novel *The*

*Diary of a Shirtwaist Striker,* Françoise Basch describes the confused but exciting events of the strike's first day. The quote within this quote (taken from Malkiel's novel) poignantly emphasizes how helpless sweatshop workers typically were—the narrator does not even know how to use a telephone:

Everywhere, work came to a stop. In the unionized workshops, one worker (male or female) blew a

*Two garment workers wear banners urging support of the Ladies Tailors strike during the 1910 general walkout.*

whistle to give the signal. More often, confusion reigned. In many shops, the girls sat down in their usual places but kept their coats on and did not move.

"We stayed whispering, and no one knowing what the other would do, not making up our minds for two hours. . . . We hardly knew where to go—or what to do next. But one of the American girls who knew how to telephone, called up the Women's Trade Union League, and they told us all to come to a big hall a few blocks away." [105]

## THE UPRISING

This call to arms led quickly to a widespread strike, involving far more workers than any previous garment-industry strike—so many, in fact, that labor historians call it "The Uprising of the Twenty Thousand." (Some estimates put the true number of strikers at twice that number or more.) The event is considered a major turning point in the garment industry labor movement and the true beginning of the women's labor movement in America.

After walking off their jobs, strikers quickly set up picket lines outside companies. This required setting up groups of union members who marched and stood outside a company's building. The strikers hoped to discourage nonunion workers from crossing the picket line and to shame others into not doing business with that company.

About seven hundred of the striking women were arrested in the walkout's early days, and over the next months many went to jail for brief periods. However, as labor organizer Morris Hillquit remarked in the *New York Call* newspaper, jail may not have been so bad: "Jail has no terror for girls who have been confined for years in workshops that are worse than prison." [106]

As more and more workers in different shops joined the strike in the next weeks, events rapidly unfolded. More and more everyday sweatshop workers became involved as the strike expanded. Union leader Grace Potter described the scene in a newspaper article:

Nearly all the available halls on the East Side have been hired by the union, Clinton Hall being general headquarters. Every day the strikers meet, grouping off so that the members from each shop talk together, planning to join them and allotting pickets for work during every hour of the day.

Now and then the tedium of this [the picket line] is relieved by revolutionary songs, most often in the Russian tongue. Or perhaps the room will be cleared for a few minutes' dance. This is often interrupted by news that girls in a new shop have gone on strike, and a call is made for volunteers to do picket duty with the inexperienced girls who have just joined the strikers' ranks. [107]

## "I WANT MY PAY"

Angry shop owners retaliated by hiring nonunion workers and threatening the women who were picketing their businesses. Many stories of bravery and courage in the face of such intimidation have been related. One is an incident described by Grace Potter:

A little girl, not more than sixteen years of age, was found leaning up against a building in West Twenty-sixth Street, sobbing and trembling violently. A group of strikers on their way to do picket duty went to her assistance but she could not speak coherently or say what had happened for quite a time. A policeman came up and waved his club.

"She has been discharged from the shop where she worked, and she is crying about that," he said. The girl did not pay any attention to him nor even notice the lie he had uttered. But when he came to her and put his hand on her arm it made her so violently hysterical that even the bluecoat seemed alarmed, and he walked rapidly away.

When she had calmed down a little she said that she was a striker. . . . A week's wage was due her, and she had been three times to the shop to get it. It was refused her each time. [Her boss] used every means he dared to frighten her. She stood her ground, however, answering all his threats with "I want my pay." Finally, enraged, the boss called up the police from the street. . . .

The police took her by the arm and shook her, and, though terrified and hysterical at his laying hands on her, she was courageous enough to resist. The boss, fearing scabs working in the shop would begin to sympathize with the child, finally gave in and paid her. As she started toward the door two men . . . took her by the arm and led her downstairs, talking to her in a way that was calculated to unnerve her, as it did.

They left her in hysterics in front of the building, and it was some time after she was found before she was strong enough to walk away. [108]

## GAINS

In the first weeks of the mass walkout, the unusual sight of "girl strikers" on picket lines amused and baffled observers around the country. Many people refused to take the female strikers seriously. However, as the women continued to picket, even during the worst of the winter snows in New York, they and their cause became increasingly credible in the public eye. One observer claimed, "Neither the police, nor the hooligan hirelings of the bosses nor the biting frost and chilling snow of December and January damped their willingness to picket the shops from early morn till late at night." [109]

The strike finally ended in the spring of 1910. Many striking workers, penniless for months and tired of being jailed repeatedly, where they were often put in the company of prostitutes and hardened criminals, felt they simply could not afford to strike any longer. As a result, only a few of the strikers' demands were met.

One positive outcome of the strike was the "Protocol of Peace," an agreement the strikers reached with many of the garment companies. A number of

## ❧ A HEROINE SUPPORTS THE STRIKERS ❧

*When contract talks between labor and management of New York cloakmaker's sweatshops broke down in 1916, the union declared a strike. Public and press support for the striking sweatshop workers was overwhelming. Helen Keller, the deaf-blind heroine of millions of Americans, was one of many celebrities moved to express publicly her support for the strikers. This excerpt is from "Why I Support the Cloakmakers," an article in the* New York Times:

I am with the cloak strikers, heart and soul, in their heroic struggle. If it were possible, I should come to New York to help them with my voice, too. I enclose a check for $200—my earnings—to be used for the strikers in the fight for better wages and a more human life.

May you remain strong and united until your battle is won. Whatever may happen, yours is the strength of a just cause. You are fighting for the right to a life better than the soul-quenching struggle for daily bread, the happiness of your children. Your courage, your enthusiasm, your perseverance are the hope of fellow workers, who bear grievous burdens. Your solidarity will help them win their battles. Let the result of this strike be what it may, the daring fight you have made will be a proud memory, an inspiration, a challenge to all who toil.

The cloakmakers are not asking for charity. They ask for a chance to live. Every dollar you contribute today will count as much as two dollars tomorrow. It will relieve want, and it will help prove to the employers that they cannot defy public sentiment. Show them that the day of cave-man ethics is past.

the larger companies refused to accept it, and bickering within the union hampered its administration over the next years. Nonetheless, the agreement was a successful blueprint for future negotiations; according to labor historian Leon Stein, it was "a model worth emulating [copying] in a time of rising industrial unrest."[110]

The Uprising had other positive results as well. It focused nationwide attention on unions and the plight of sweatshop workers. Also, membership of the WTUL jumped from about one thousand before the strike to about nineteen thousand afterwards.

## "70,000 ZEROS"

Perhaps the strike's biggest result, however, was that it proved that even the poorest and humblest garment workers could fight for their rights. It therefore gained enormous symbolic

*Members of the International Ladies Garment Workers stage a massive walkout in 1929.*

significance, providing hope to an army of previously anonymous laborers. Abraham Liessen, a prominent Yiddish poet, wrote an often-repeated line (with a little poetic license in the figures) that reflected this dramatic effect: "The 70,000 zeros became 70,000 fighters." [111]

In the aftermath of the Uprising, other successful sweatshop-related strikes were held, including major garment worker strikes in Philadelphia, Chicago, Rochester, and Cleveland. Throughout the 1910s and 1920s, unions became steadily more stable and powerful.

Labor unions were not the only source of aid and support for sweatshop workers, however. Members of the middle and upper classes who were dedicated to social reform also provided significant help.

# CHAPTER 6

# THE REFORMERS AND THE SWEATSHOPS

As labor unions were dramatically changing for the better the working lives of tens of thousands of sweatshop employees, another social force was affecting their everyday lives. This was a movement that swept America in the early decades of the twentieth century and aimed to provide serious social reform.

This social reform movement hoped to make life better for all Americans, but reformers had a special interest in the disadvantaged, and most especially in sweatshop workers. Reformers had an almost religious belief that many of society's ills could be cured through commonsense measures and basic health standards. Writer Luc Sante noted, "Sunlight, air, and the eradication of filth are for [them] the agents that will drive out crime, disease, illiteracy, inertia, and despair." [112]

Individually, these reformers were associated with a wide variety of political, religious, and social groups. Collectively, however, they were frequently called Progressives. Historian Otis Pease defined the term when he wrote that Progressivism involved more than simply creating new roads or buildings: "To talk of progress in America in 1900 was to talk of material improvements; but to call a man 'progressive' was to label him a reformer, a man determined to improve his society, revise its laws, purify its politics, rearrange its economic awards, and invigorate its morals." [113]

## "SOMETHING FOR THE NEEDY"

Reformers generally did not come from the working class, as did sweatshop workers; most came from the middle class. They typically had grown up with a strong sense of social duty, and they carried this sense into their adult lives.

## ❧ TEA AT THE COLONY CLUB ❧

*On occasion, "allies"—high-society women sympathetic to the cause of organized labor —held meetings at which their upper-crust friends could mingle with the working class. This report, from the* Call, *December 16, 1909, describes a tea given in honor of garment strikers at New York City's exclusive Colony Club. The term "the 400" refers to the elite of New York society. The piece is reprinted in Leon Stein's* Out of the Sweatshop:

A remarkable meeting, one that was as peculiar as it was interesting, and as unique as it was pathetic, took place yesterday afternoon for the striking waistmakers at the Colony Club, the most exclusive club in the city, of which Miss Anne Morgan, Miss Elizabeth Marbury, Mrs. Edgerton, Mrs. J.B. Harriman and others of the same financial and social standing are members.

These women, the cream of the "400," had come to listen to the story of the strike from the lips of the strikers, told in simple words by those who had been mistreated, abused, enslaved by capitalism, poverty and police per-secution. Four hundred women, representing the richest people of the world, occupied as many gilt chairs in the beautiful gymnasium of the sumptuous club.

In contradistinction to this bejeweled, befurred, belaced, begowned audience, Miss Mary E. Dreier, president of the Women's Trade Union League, brought with her 10 of the girl strikers, 10 wage slaves, some of them mere children, who, as they subsequently told, worked from early morning till late at night for as little as $3 a week; girls on whose meagre earnings depended children still younger, mothers sick and fathers out of work.

And the rich women listened. Seldom, if ever, have they listened with such interest to the tales of the war between capital and labor, to the incidents of pain, of misery, of grief in the great struggle between the classes.

Miss Dreier, introducing the strikers, said that she would not give their names, as some of them had to tell of circumstances too painful to appear in print.

Eleanor Roosevelt, a leading reformer and the wife of Franklin D. Roosevelt, once commented on the obligations of such a background. She said that being raised with a sense of social duty meant "you were kind to the poor, you did not neglect your philanthropic [charitable] duties, you assisted the hospitals and did something for the needy."[114]

A few reformers came from wealthy families and privileged backgrounds— the very highest level of society. These people of means grew up leading lives that included such luxuries as private schools, households with servants—and protection from understanding how different, and difficult, life was for sweatshop workers.

As adults, some wealthy people remained oblivious to or uninterested in the problems of the working class. Others, however, gained awareness and empathy—especially after the startling wake-up calls of such front-page news stories as violent strikes and tragic fires. Historian Otis Pease notes that for these well-off men and women "the misery of the factory family's three-room tenement flat twelve blocks away [came] as a shocking and galvanizing revelation." [115]

## THE ALLIES

Whether wealthy or simply comfortable, many members of the middle and upper classes—typically women,

*Eleanor Roosevelt listens attentively during a lecture. She was a leading reformer.*

often single—became reformers. They tried to help sweatshop workers any way they could. Sweatshop workers who were active in union organizing called these reformers "allies."

In many cases the allies provided real help. They raised or donated money for causes such as strike funds (which gave workers a sustenance wage while striking). Others donated

their time and expertise; lawyers and doctors, for instance, offered professional help that would otherwise have been out of the reach of sweatshop workers.

However, the help was not always effective—or welcome. Many workers disliked and distrusted these well-meaning people, feeling that the allies were simply controlling do-gooders

---

## ✑ "DESPERATE REALITY" ✑

*Bessie Van Vorst was one of many middle-class women who left their comfortable lives for a while in order to experience the hardships of the sweatshop firsthand. She went from her home in New York to Pittsburgh in 1902 to work in a pickle-canning factory, adopting the name Esther Kelley. Her account is excerpted in Barbara Mayer Wertheimer's* We Were There: The Story of Working Women in America:

[I and other women set out to] discover and adopt their [working women's] point of view, put ourselves in their surroundings, assume their burdens, unite with them in their daily effort . . . to give a faithful picture of things as they exist, both in and out of the factory, and to suggest remedies that occurred to me as practical. My desire is to act as a mouthpiece for the women labourer. . . .

Before leaving New York I assumed my disguise. . . . With the aid of coarse woolen garments, a shabby felt sailor hat, a cheap piece of fur, a knitted shawl

and gloves I am transformed into a working girl of the ordinary type.

After her first day at work she wrote:

I have become with desperate reality a factory girl, alone, inexperienced, friendless. I am making $4.20 a week and spending $3 of this for board alone, and I dread not being strong enough to keep my job. . . .

My hands are stiff, my thumbs almost blistered. . . . Cases are emptied and refilled; bottles are labeled, stamped and rolled away . . . and still there are more cases, more jars, more bottles. Oh! the monotony of it . . . ! Now and then someone cuts a finger or runs a splinter under the flesh . . . and still the work goes on. Once I pause an instant, my head dazed and weary, my ears strained to bursting with the deafening noise. Quickly a voice whispers in my ear: "You'd better not stand there doin' nothin'. If *she* catches you she'll give it to you."

whose organizations were ineffective shams. Union organizer Leonora O'Reilly summed up the feelings of many when she commented, "Contact with the Lady does harm in the long run. It gives the wrong standard."[116]

Workers often called allies disdainful names such as "the mink brigade" or "the high-society ladies." Theresa S. Malkiel, in her autobiographical novel *The Diary of a Shirtwaist Striker,* has her protagonist muse, "I shouldn't wonder that their conscience pricks them a bit—they must be ashamed of being fortune children while so many of the girls have never known what a good day means. The rich women seem to be softer than the men; perhaps it's because they ain't making the money—they're only spending it."[117]

Some labor organizers felt especially uncomfortable with financial aid from very wealthy patrons, whom they found insincere and untrustworthy. When socialite Alva Belmont offered her lavish mansion as collateral to bail out jailed strikers in 1909, for instance, the famous anarchist Emma Goldman commented coldly,

> If the strike is won, it will be on its merits, not because it was assisted by wealthy ladies. I have no personal feelings against Mrs. Belmont or Miss Morgan [Anne Morgan, another prominent ally and the daughter of millionaire financier J.P. Morgan], but their contributions will not harmonize

capital and labor. They will harm the labor movement, which, to be successful, must be entirely independent.[118]

## SETTLEMENT HOUSES

Despite this distrust, and the fact that some "high-society ladies" were indeed interested mostly in fashionable self-sacrifice, a tremendous amount of good did come to sweatshop workers as a result of the reform movement. The element of reform that perhaps did the most good for the greatest number of workers was the settlement house. Historian Moses Rischin writes, "Of the many institutions that showed the social concern of upper-class reformers, few carried the commitment of the settlements."[119]

Settlement houses combined aspects of social service agencies—a virtually unknown concept in those days—with what would now be called community centers. Their staffs were dedicated to providing a wide range of services to specific neighborhoods.

Staff members typically lived where they worked, as part of their commitment to the neighborhood. Moses Rischin comments, "Settlement workers took up full-time residence in the tenements, sharing the food, the filth, the noise, and the heartache."[120]

The overall emphasis was on supporting the Americanization of newcomers by teaching them language,

*Girls at a settlement house learn to cook. Settlement houses helped immigrants learn to be Americans.*

civics, and other tools that would help them find better jobs. However, the goal was to include in one service health and home care, schooling and recreation, culture and politics. The range of activities thus included nurse visits to poor families, the sponsorship of athletic teams and special-interest groups, and classes on such subjects as housekeeping, hygiene, art, music, and crafts.

Settlement houses often grew large enough to encompass such features as day nurseries, gyms, community kitchens, community theaters, and boarding houses. The largest incorporated playgrounds and even rural camps where inner-city children could explore nature.

## "NOT STRANGE BUT NATURAL"

In time many settlement houses became much more than simple neighborhood centers. They also served as magnets for a wide range of reformers, teachers, and social workers. These people came to various settlement houses from around the country, and even the world, to learn, help, and teach.

The most famous settlement house, and one of the first in America, was Hull House, situated in a working-class immigrant neighborhood of Chicago.

Founded in 1889 by social work pioneer Jane Addams, Hull House was widely admired and copied, and by 1910 there were about four hundred similar houses across the country. In her autobiography, Addams reflected on her reasons for founding the center. She wrote,

In those early days we were often asked why we had come to live on Halsted Street when we could afford to live somewhere else. I remember one man who used to shake his head and say it was "the strangest thing he had met in his experience," but who was finally convinced that it was "not strange but natural."

In time it came to seem natural to all of us that the Settlement should be there. If it is natural to feed the hungry and care for the sick, it is certainly natural to give pleasure to the young, comfort to the aged, and to minister to the deep-seated craving for social intercourse that all men feel. [121]

*A view of the exterior of Chicago's Hull House, the most famous settlement house.*

## "A NEW WORLD OPENS FOR US"

In addition to organizations like settlement houses, another arm of the reform movement concentrated on improving, by direct action, the physical health of sweatshop workers. Public health agencies run by the government were often inadequate for (or uninterested in) the requirements of immigrant workers. As a result, reformers frequently sponsored nurses and doctors who made house calls to working-class tenements.

One of the most prominent of these was Lillian Wald, a nurse who founded New York's Henry Street Settlement House. The child of a comfortable middle-class family, Wald devoted herself to healing and teaching the basics of health education to poor tenement dwellers. Every day Wald threw herself with robust vigor into the midst of squalor and disease. She noted her typical reaction when she encountered a place that needed help:

I came with very little program of what could or should be done. I went into every room in the front and rear tenements, set the dwellers to sweeping, cleaning, and burning the refuse. In some rooms swill thrown on the floor, vessels [chamberpots] standing unemptied after the night's use. I saw the housekeeper, who promised cooperation in keeping the place cleaner, and I impressed on her that I would repeat the rounds next day and frequently thereafter.

Writer and historian Irving Howe commented that Wald's tasks seemed endless, and listed a typical caseload:

Children with summer bowel complaints that sent infant mortality rates soaring; children with measles, unquarantined; children "scarred with vermin bites"; a case of "puerperal septicaemia [infection after childbirth], lying on a vermin-infested bed without sheets or pillow-cases"; a pregnant mother with a crippled child and two others living on chunks of dry bread sent in by neighbors; people "ill from organic trouble and also from poor food." [122]

Ruth Cohen was one of the thousands of sweatshop workers whose lives were touched by Lillian Wald and her coworker, Mary Brewster. Cohen, who had been seriously ill, wrote in a diary,

Miss Wald comes to our house, and a new world opens for us. We recommend to her all our neighbours who are in need. The children join clubs in the Nurses' Settlement and I spend a great deal of time there. Miss Wald and Miss Brewster treat me with affectionate kindness. I am being

*A public health nurse concludes a home visit to a mother and her two children.*

fed up [given good nourishment]. I am to be sent to the country for health, for education.[123]

## "BABY SICK INSIDE"

In 1904 a reporter for the *Jewish Forward* described the typical rounds of another slum nurse as she visited a tenement mother and provided some basic tips on hygiene. The reporter wrote:

There is never any fresh air in these rooms, it is hard to imagine how people can live there, but they do.

The nurse finds two babies on the bed, six-month-old twins. An eighteen-month-old baby sits on the floor chewing on paper. The nurse takes a card out of her satchel and starts to question the woman; the latter doesn't know much English, but one of the girls who had come in when the nurse arrived is ready to answer for her. The nurse asks how many windows are in the apartment, how many people live there. She writes everything on the card. Then she examines the babies. One of the twins has a banana in its mouth; the other is battling with a big pear.

"You mustn't give the babies such things," she tells the mother. When the girl interprets to the woman she gets angry: "What's her business? I'm not spending her money!"

The nurse talks directly to the mother: "Baby sick inside," pointing to her stomach. "Sick here, in the belly."

"No sick," says the mother. "Babies all right."

The nurse asks the girl to make clear to the woman that bananas will make her babies sick. The woman nods her head. Then she learns that the mother is using condensed milk, and that is no good. The mother waves her hands in despair and points to her bosom: "I ain't got none."

The nurse writes down what kind of milk to buy, and where to get it. She instructs the mother to wash the babies two to three times a day in hot weather, in salt water. The mother is warned not to drink beer or tea, it makes babies sick inside. Drink milk, cocoa, or water. She should keep the babies outside [in the fresh air].[124]

## IMPROVING THE QUALITY OF LIFE

Health was not the only aspect of the overall quality of life in which reform efforts helped sweatshop workers. Another focus was on improving educational opportunities.

In 1890 Jacob Riis described a key part of the problem: Workers who began at an early age and slaved all day simply had no time for school. Riis wrote, "There are whole settlements on this East Side [of New York] where English is practically an unknown tongue, though the people be both willing and anxious to learn. 'When shall we find time to learn?' asked one of them of me once. I owe him the answer yet."[125]

In the next decades, however, the situation improved dramatically. Thanks to intense efforts by reformers, by 1910 most states required that children attend school until the age of sixteen. Educational quality also improved, thanks to such reforms as better-trained and better paid teachers and longer school years.

The daily lives of workers were also directly improved by the creation of clean, safe places where they and their families could enjoy free, healthy recreation. Thousands of public parks, playgrounds, swimming pools, libraries, and other centers were developed with this in mind. Typically these places were financed by wealthy philanthropists. Steel baron Andrew Carnegie, for instance, used part of his vast fortune to build thousands of public libraries across the country.

The Carnegie libraries allowed even the poorest sweatshop worker to enjoy a lifelong education, and they proved enduringly popular. Samuel Tenenbaum, who grew up in a New York tenement, recalled his favorite childhood hangout: "In other neighborhoods, the ice cream parlor, the poolroom, the dance hall were the favorite gathering places. In Brownsville [a neighborhood in Brooklyn], it was the library on Glenmore and Watkins avenues. There we got to know one another, there we argued about books and writers, there we made intellectual discoveries."[126]

## THE MUCKRAKERS

Reformers knew that if their movement was to become more than simply the work of a few dedicated individuals, they needed the backing of the public. They found the publicity they needed, in part, through some of the reform movement's best-known public advocates. One was Jacob Riis, whose tireless work as a photojournalist earned him the nickname "Emancipator of the Slums." Photographer Lewis Hine

*A portrait of photojournalist Jacob Riis. Riis's work brought national attention to the plight of the sweatshop worker.*

was another journalist who brought to light such topics as the horrors of child labor.

Riis and Hine were associated with a loose affiliation of writers known as muckrakers. Today these journalists would be called investigative reporters. They provided the public with in-depth, often harrowing accounts of the hardships suffered by sweatshop workers.

## ❧ "A GREAT ALLIED LABOR OF NEEDLEWORK" ☙

*The novelist Theodore Dreiser was one of many writers associated with the "muckrakers," crusading journalists who exposed the tragedies of sweatshop life. This passage, reprinted in Stein's* Out of the Sweatshop, *is from an article Dreiser wrote in the early 1920s:*

Men, women and children are daily making coats, vests, knee-pants and trousers. There are side branches of overalls, cloaks, hats, caps, suspenders, jerseys and blouses. Some make dresses and waists, underwear and neckwear, waistbands, skirts, shirts and purses; still others, fur, or fur trimmings, feathers and artificial flowers, umbrellas, and even collars. It is all a great allied labor of needlework, done by machine and finishing work done by hand. . . . [They] support a vast number of] infants, school children, aged parents, and physically disabled relatives. . . . You may go throughout New York and Brooklyn, and wherever you find a neighborhood poor enough you will find those workers. They occupy the very worst of tumbledown dwellings.

The most prominent magazine associated with muckraking was *McClure's*. It came to fame by publishing explosive exposés by such pioneering writers as Ida Tarbell, Lincoln Steffens, and Ray Stannard Baker. These and other muckraking journalists were joined by a number of like-minded novelists, including Upton Sinclair, whose best-selling 1906 novel *The Jungle* shocked the nation by realistically depicting the horrors of the Chicago meatpacking industry.

As a group, muckrakers had a strong sense of moral outrage. They believed that they had an obligation to uncover injustice, and that the public likewise had an obligation to help the disadvantaged when confronted with the facts. The publisher of *McClure's* wrote,

"Capitalists, workingmen, politicians, citizens—all breaking the law, or letting it be broken. Who is left to uphold it? . . . There is no one left; none but all of us. . . . We have to pay in the end, every one of us."[127]

### "THE BRUTES"

In the 1920s the worst offenders among the sweatshops began to close down, in large part because of the successful efforts of unions and reformers. Sweatshop workers' lives gradually became safer, better, and healthier.

Permanent change was slow to come, however, because government remained largely opposed to strict regulations regarding workers and workplaces. The fact that such regulations did eventually become law is mainly because many politicians came to embrace the reform movement.

One leading political reformer was Theodore Roosevelt, who energetically backed many reform efforts during a career that included two terms as U.S. president. Roosevelt once commented, "No hard-and-fast rule can be laid down as to the way in which [reform] must be done; but most certainly every man, whatever his position, should strive to do it in some way and to some degree."[128]

In addition to his professional interest in reform, Roosevelt strongly empathized on a personal basis. The *New York Times* reported that when he visited a group of strikers in 1913, Roosevelt was deeply touched by a story told to him by a fifteen-year-old Italian garment worker:

"At the end of her narrative she said with a catch in her voice: 'If only they would let us sing while we work.'

'The brutes,' Mr. Roosevelt muttered under his breath, 'to prevent them from singing if they can be cheerful under such conditions.'"[129]

## LEGACY OF THE REFORMERS

In the last years of the sweatshop era, new state and federal laws directly improving the lives of sweatshop workers were passed. Among these was stringent legislation requiring improvements in tenement construction and maintenance. Historian Otis Pease writes, "At the dead center of

the urban reformer's consciousness stood the modern slum. No feature of American life in the new century more starkly silhouetted poverty against the hopeful backdrop of progress."[130]

Many child labor, workplace safety, and fire laws were also passed—and, just as important, enforced. For example, New York City and other cities significantly revised their factory building safety codes. Frances Perkins, who

*Theodore Roosevelt backed many reforms during his presidency that dramatically improved the lot of the sweatshop worker.*

served as one of the chief investigators for the New York State commission assembled after the Triangle fire, recalled that direct action was needed to convince some authorities about passing new legislation:

> We saw to it that [they] got up at dawn and drove with us for an unannounced visit to a Cattaraugus County cannery and that they saw with their own eyes the little children, not adolescents, but five-, six-, and seven-year-olds, snipping beans and shelling peas. We made sure that they saw the machinery that would scalp a girl or cut off a man's arm. Hours so long that both men and women were depleted and exhausted became realities to them through seeing for themselves the dirty little factories. [131]

## MORE CHANGES

In the following years many states followed New York's lead and adopted stricter measures. The federal government, however, was slower to respond. It did not establish basic standards for child labor, for instance, until 1938. It was not until the 1930s, as well, that the federal government began regulating other aspects of job rights, such as minimum wage, workman's compensation, unemployment benefits, and the five-day, forty-hour workweek.

Blatant exploitation of workers in sweatshops would reappear periodically, in America and abroad, in later decades. However, the era of the "classic" sweatshop—the cramped tenement apartment or factory filled with desperately poor immigrants—drew to a close as did the Industrial Revolution.

# NOTES

## INTRODUCTION: THE SWEATSHOP IN THE INDUSTRIAL REVOLUTION

1. Jacob A. Riis, *How the Other Half Lives.* New York: Penguin Books, 1997, p. 96.
2. Leon Stein, ed., *Out of the Sweatshop: The Struggle for Industrial Democracy.* New York: Quadrangle, 1977, p. xv.

## CHAPTER 1: WHO WORKED IN SWEATSHOPS?

3. Riis, *How the Other Half Lives,* p. 93.
4. Quoted in Susan A. Glenn, *Daughters of the Shtetl: Life and Labor in the Immigrant Generation.* Ithaca, NY: Cornell University Press, 1990, p. 2.
5. Quoted in Glenn, *Daughters of the Shtetl,* p. 50.
6. Quoted in Irving Howe, *World of Our Fathers: The Journey of the East European Jews to America and the Life They Found and Made.* New York: Schocken Books, 1990, p. 43.
7. Quoted in Howe, *World of Our Fathers,* p. 408.
8. Rose Cohen, *Out of the Shadow: A Russian Jewish Girlhood on the Lower East Side.* Ithaca, NY: Cornell University Press, 1995, p. 71.
9. Moses Rischin, *The Promised City: New York's Jews 1870–1914.* New York: Harper and Row, 1970, p. 51.
10. Frederic C. Howe, "The City: Hope of Democracy," in Otis Pease, ed., *The Progressive Years: The Spirit and Achievement of American Reform.* New York: George Braziller, 1962, p. 27.
11. Ray Stannard Baker, in Stein, *Out of the Sweatshop,* p. 22.
12. Oscar Theodore Barck Jr. and Nelson Manfred Blake, *Since 1900.* New York: Macmillan, 1965, p. 12.
13. Quoted in Glenn, *Daughters of the Shtetl,* p. 59.
14. Quoted in Sydney Stahl Weinberg, *The World of Our Mothers: The Lives of Jewish Immigrant Women.* New York: Schocken Books, 1988, p. 97.
15. Frank Freidel, *America in the Twentieth Century.* New York: Knopf, 1960, p. 47.
16. Rischin, *The Promised City,* p. 95.
17. Quoted in Glenn, *Daughters of the Shtetl,* p. 110.
18. Quoted in Glenn, *Daughters of the Shtetl,* p. 83.
19. Quoted in Weinberg, *The World of Our Mothers,* p. 190.

20. Louise C. Odencrantz, "The Italian Seamstress," in Stein, *Out of the Sweatshop,* p. 62.

21. Riis, *How the Other Half Lives,* p. 95.

22. Pauline Newman, "Letters to Michael and Hugh," *The Triangle Factory Fire,* Cornell University Library. www.ilr.cornell.edu.

23. Quoted in Stein, *Out of the Sweatshop,* p. 127.

## CHAPTER 2: DAILY LIFE IN A SWEATSHOP

24. Barbara Mayer Wertheimer, *We Were There: The Story of Working Women in America.* New York: Pantheon, 1977, p. 295.

25. Rischin, *The Promised City,* p. 66.

26. Daniel Soyer, *Sweatshops in the New York Garment Industry: The Jewish Era, ca. 1880–ca. 1920.* Unpublished paper for The Sweatshop Project—a Rockefeller Foundation Humanities Institute sponsored by the Lower East Side Tenement Museum and UNITE, 1997, p. 26.

27. Riis, *How the Other Half Lives,* p. 85.

28. Clara Lemlich, "Life in the Shop," *New York Evening Journal,* November 28, 1909, *The Triangle Factory Fire,* Cornell University Library. www.ilr.cornell.edu/trianglefire/texts/stein_ootss/oots s_cl.html.

29. Lemlich, "Life in the Shop."

30. Quoted in Barbara Mayer Wertheimer, *We Were There: The Story of Working Women in America.* New York: Pantheon, 1977, p. 295.

31. Cohen, *Out of the Shadow,* pp. 81–82.

32. Cohen, *Out of the Shadow,* p. 121.

33. Sadie Frowne, "Days and Dreams," *The Independent,* September 25, 1902, *The Triangle Factory Fire,* Cornell University Library. www.ilr.cornell.edu/trianglefire/texts/stein_ootss/oo tss_cl.html.

34. Cohen, *Out of the Shadow,* p. 83.

35. Quoted in Irving Howe and Kenneth Libo, *How We Lived: A Documentary History of Immigrant Jews in America 1880–1930.* New York: Richard Marek Publishers, 1979, p. 136.

36. Quoted in Howe and Libo, *How We Lived,* p. 153.

37. Françoise Basch, in Theresa S. Malkiel, *The Diary of a Shirtwaist Striker.* Ithaca, NY: ILR Press/Cornell University, 1990, p. 16.

38. Newman, "Letters to Michael and Hugh."

39. Quoted in Glenn, *Daughters of the Shtetl,* p. 151.

40. Quoted in Howe and Libo, *How We Lived,* p. 153.

41. Quoted in Wertheimer, *We Were There,* pp. 223–24.

42. Meyer London, "Survival of the Meanest," in Stein, *Out of the Sweatshop,* p. 98.

# GLOSSARY

**axon:** An extension of a neuron that carries nerve impulses to other cells.

**brain stem:** The section of the brain that includes the medulla oblongata, pons, and midbrain.

**cerebellum:** The portion of the brain that controls movements.

**cerebrospinal fluid:** A clear fluid formed in the ventricles of the brain that bathes the brain and spinal cord.

**cerebrum:** The uppermost portion of the brain that is in charge of higher mental functions.

**dendrite:** An extension of a neuron that receives nerve impulses from other cells.

**diencephalon:** The middle portion of the brain that contains the thalamus and hypothalamus.

**electroencephalogram (EEG):** A recording of the electrical activity of brain waves.

**enzyme:** A protein that speeds up chemical reactions within a cell.

**gray matter:** The area of the central nervous system that lacks myelin.

**limbic system:** Several interrelated areas in the brain that work together to produce emotions.

**magnetic resonance imaging (MRI):** A technique for visualizing internal structures using energy released by magnetic fields.

**meninges:** Membranes that cover the brain and spinal cord.

**myelin:** Fatty material that provides a sheath-like cover on some neurons.

**neuron:** A cell specialized to generate and carry electrical impulses in the body.

**neuroglia:** Tissue composed of cells that nourish and support neurons.

**neurotransmitter:** A chemical secreted at the axon end of a neuron that carries an impulse across a synapse.

**receptor cell:** Sensory cell that can detect and transmit sensory stimuli.

**sensory adaptation:** A reduction in the rate at which nerve impulses are generated by sensory receptors that are exposed to continuous stimulation.

**synapse:** The gap between a neuron and another cell that is bridged by a neurotransmitter.

**ventricles:** Spaces within the brain.

**vitreous humor:** Gel-like fluid that fills the anterior chamber of the eye.

**white matter:** The area of the central nervous system that contains myelin.

# FOR FURTHER READING

## Books

Jim Barmeier, *The Brain*. San Diego, CA: Lucent Books, 1996. This book reviews historical and current understanding of brain structure, memory, sleep, diseases, and treatments.

Charles B. Clayman, *The Brain and Nervous System*. Pleasantville, NY: Reader's Digest Association, 1991. This book provides general information on anatomy and functions of the nervous system, including consciousness and sleep.

Jack Fincher, *The Brain*. Washington, DC: U.S. News Books, nd. After reviewing brain anatomy and function, this book focuses on how drugs affect the brain.

Alma Guinness, *ABC's of the Human Body*. Pleasantville, NY: Reader's Digest Association, 1987. This book discusses the various structures of the human body and addresses some interesting reasons for certain body functions.

The Handy Science Answer Book. Canton, MI: Visible Ink Press, 1997. This book gives good explanations for a variety of happenings in the science world.

*How in the World?* Pleasantville, NY: Reader's Digest Association, 1990. This book provides interesting coverage of both physical and biological events that occur in life.

David E. Larson, *Mayo Clinic Family Health Book*. New York: William Morrow, 1996. This book describes in simple terms the many diseases that can affect the human body.

Susan McKeever, *The Dorling Kindersley Science Encyclopedia*. New York: Dorling Kindersley, 1994. This encyclopedia gives concise information on physical and biological occurrences in life. Good illustrations help to explain topics.

Mary Lou Mulvihill, *Human Diseases*. Norwalk, CT: Appleton and Lange, 1995. This book provides a good description of the most common diseases of the human body.

Lael Wertenbaker, *The Eye*. Washington, DC: U.S. News Books, nd. A comprehensive explanation of the eye and its functions.

*World Book Medical Encyclopedia.* Chicago: World Book, 1995. This encyclopedia provides a vast amount of information on the physiology of human body systems.

## Websites

**Countdown for Kids Magazine** (www.jdf.org). Students can research any topic that interests them, including health and medicine.

**Fact Monster, Learning** (www.factmonster.com). This website provides information on a wide variety of topics and has a good science encyclopedia.

**Neuroscience for Kids** (http://faculty.washington.edu) Information, experiments, activities, and research links on the nervous system are available at this site.

**Yucky Kids** (www.nj.com). Easy-to-read articles on the nervous system and other body systems.

# WORKS CONSULTED

## Books

Robert Berkow, *The Merck Manual of Medical Information.* New York: Pocket Books, 1997. Provides a detailed explanation of all organs. This book gives information on the causes, symptoms, diagnosis, and treatment of many diseases.

*Brain Facts: A Primer on the Brain and Nervous System.* Washington, DC: Society for Neuroscience, 1993. Outlines the physiology of parts of the nervous system and presents current knowledge on memory, sleep, and diseases of the nervous system.

Charlotte Dienhart, *Basic Human Anatomy and Physiology.* Philadelphia: W.B. Saunders, 1979. This textbook covers the structure and function of all organ systems in the human body. It also provides information on symptoms and treatments of various diseases.

William C. Goldberg, *Clinical Physiology Made Ridiculously Simple.* Miami: Med Masters, 1995. This booklet gives a detailed explanation of body systems. Illustrations reinforce the written content.

John Hole Jr., *Essentials of Human Anatomy and Physiology.* Dubuque, IA: Wm. C. Brown, 1992. This textbook of anatomy and physiology provides detailed explanations of the structure and function of all human body systems.

Anthony L. Komaroff, *Harvard Medical School Family Health Guide.* New York: Simon and Schuster, 1999. This book provides comprehensive coverage of the various disorders and diseases that can affect the human body. Symptoms, causes, diagnosis, and treatment options are provided.

Ann Kramer, *The Human Body. The World Book Encyclopedia of Science.* Chicago: World Book, 1987. This book provides information on all body systems and gives explanations about unusual and interesting events that occur in the human body.

Peretz Lavie, *The Enchanted World of Sleep.* New Haven and London: Yale University Press, 1996. The author explains current and past studies on sleep, giving the reader a complete picture of sleep research.

Stanley Loeb, *The Illustrated Guide to Diagnostic Tests.* Springhouse, PA: Springhouse Corporation, 1994. This medical book gives a thorough description and explanation of how and why medical technologies are employed to diagnose and treat human diseases and disorders.

Elaine Marieb, *Human Anatomy and Physiology.* Redwood City, CA: Benjamin/Cummings, 1995. This book offers a detailed explanation of all human body structures and organs.

Lawrence Pool, *Nature's Masterpiece: The Brain and How It Works.* New York: Walker, 1987. This book contains concise descriptions of each part of the brain and the roles neurosurgeons play in advancing the knowledge of brain function.

Richard Restak, *The Brain.* New York: Bantam Books, 1984. Based on the PBS television series of the same name, this book provides a comprehensive review of brain structure and function.

———, *Receptors.* New York: Bantam Books, 1994. This book describes recent scientific advances in mapping brain function and research on the effects of drugs on brain cells.

## Websites

**About** (www.about.com). This is an easy-to-use website that offers information on a wide variety of topics, including health and medicine.

**American Association of Neurological Surgeons** (www.neuro surgery.org). This website describes research and treatments for patients with brain tumors.

**CDC** (www.cdc.gov). This website contains information from the Centers for Disease Control and Prevention on any topic in health.

**Clinical Implications** (www.nobel.se). This website contains drawings and photographs along with information on all medical topics.

**Cornell Medical College** (www.edcenter.med.cornell.edu). The medical college of Cornell provides a wide range of information on body systems.

**11th Hour** (www.blackwellscience.com). This is a valuable resource for any type of information in science. To find information on the nervous system, go to "Introduction to Biology."

**JAMA HIV AIDS Resource Center** (www.ama–assn.org). The *Journal of the American Medical Association,* published by the American Medical Association, is a great resource for any topic in medicine.

**Michigan Parkinson Foundation** (http://parkinsonsmi.org). The Parkinson Foundation of Michigan gives a good overview of what Parkinson's disease is, who gets it, the symptoms and treatments, and how to cope with the disease.

**MSN Search** (www.search.msn.com). This website provides a science library suitable for most students.

**New England Neurological Associates** (www.neneuro.com). This website provides the latest advances in neurosurgery and explains how brain tumors can be treated by microsurgery, laser techniques, and radioactive implants.

**The Merck Manual Web Site** (www.merck.com). This website gives a detailed explanation of body systems and diseases.

## Internet Sources

American Heart Association, "Stroke Treatment Advances," 2000. www.americanheart.org.

Dr. Koop Lifecare Corporation, "Robotics and Surgery of the Brain and Spinal Cord," April 11, 2000. www.drkoop.com.

Encarta Online Encyclopedia, "Coma," November 4, 2001. http://encarta.msn.com.

Gale Encyclopedia of Medicine, "Cerebrospinal Fluid Analysis." www.findarticles.com.

———, "Electrical Stimulation of the Brain." www.findarticles.com.

———, "Evoked Potential Studies." www.findarticles.com.

Health Alliance, "World's First Optimized Stereotactic Radiotherapy System in the Neuroscience Institute at the University Hospital of Cincinnati," August 5, 2001. www.techmall.com.

How Stuff Works, "How Magnetic Resonance Imaging Works," 2001. www.howstuffworks.com.

———, "How Robotic Surgery Will Work." 2001. www.howstuff works.com.

International Radiosurgery Support Association, "A Typical Treatment Day: Information on Gamma Knife and Linac Stereotactic Radiosurgery for Brain Tumors," 2000. www.irsa.org.

Methodist Health Care System, "Infectious Diseases," 2001. www.methodisthealth.com.

New York State Department of Health Communicable Disease Fact Sheet, "Tetanus," February 1999. www.health.state.ny.us.

Society for Neuroscience, "Brain Imaging," 1996. www.sfn.org.

# INDEX

# PICTURE CREDITS

# ABOUT THE AUTHORS

Both Pam Walker and Elaine Wood have degrees in biology and education from colleges in Georgia. They have taught science in grades seven through twelve since the mid–1980s. Ms. Walker and Ms. Wood are coauthors of more than a dozen resource and activity books for science teachers and two science textbooks.